Chuck Davison

Please return

ARNOLD'S
BODYBUILDING FOR MEN

By Arnold Schwarzenegger

With Bill Dobbins

ARNOLD'S
BODYBUILDING FOR MEN
By Arnold Schwarzenegger

With Bill Dobbins

SIMON AND SCHUSTER · NEW YORK

Also by Arnold Schwarzenegger

ARNOLD: EDUCATION OF A BODYBUILDER
  (with Douglas Kent Hall)
ARNOLD'S BODYSHAPING FOR WOMEN
  (with Douglas Kent Hall)

Also by Bill Dobbins

GOLD'S GYM WEIGHT TRAINING BOOK

Published by Simon and Schuster
A Division of Gulf & Western Corporation
Simon & Schuster Building
1230 Avenue of the Americas
New York, New York 10020
SIMON AND SCHUSTER and colophon are trademarks of Simon & Schuster
Designed by Martin Moskof & Assoc. Inc./Sharon Stein
Manufactured in the United States of America
10 9 8 7 6 5 4 3 2 1

Library of Congress Cataloging in Publication Data

Schwarzenegger, Arnold.
   Arnold's Bodybuilding for men.
   1. Bodybuilding.   I. Dobbins, Bill, date, joint author.
II. Title.   III. Title: Bodybuilding for men.
GV546.5.S38   646.7'5   80-28764

ISBN 0-671-25613-0

For my mother,

for Jim Lorimer—an invaluable friend and professional
associate who has been instrumental in making the country
aware of the full value of weight resistance training,

and a special thanks to John Balik, Peter Brenner, Albert
Busek, Caruso, Neal Nordlinger, Joe Weider, Art Zeller, and
Roy Zurkowski for their generous assistance in making this
book possible.

CONTENTS

INTRODUCTION
A New Kind of Training

"Didn't you used to be Arnold Schwarzenegger?" asked my old friend. He was joking, of course, referring to the fact that, although I still train at World Gym in Santa Monica and try to stay in excellent shape, I am no longer a competitive bodybuilder. All of us in the gym laughed at this remark, but it made me pause for a moment and take stock.

My life has changed drastically since 1975 when I won my sixth Mr. Olympia title and retired from competition. Until then, training had completely dominated my life. It *was* my life. Four hours a day spent in mind-blowing sessions with the weights, everything from the way I ate and slept to my social life entirely geared to winning bodybuilding championships.

But that is now in the past. I have always thrived on challenges and, once it became too easy to win bodybuilding contests and victory had become predictable, I decided to look around for new worlds to conquer. So now I make my living as an actor, an author and a businessman. I buy and sell real estate, give lectures at universities, write books, hold seminars, promote the World Championships of Bodybuilding, work as a television commentator and appear on numerous radio and television talk shows. My activities demand that I travel tens of thousands of miles each year—to Europe, Australia, Africa, and virtually every corner of the globe. Yet, despite the fact that I have such a hectic schedule, a lot of people think that I, somehow, have access to more hours in the day than they do, and am able to find the time to stay in shape that is not available to them.

"It's different for you," they will tell me. "After all, you are a professional athlete, a bodybuilder. But I'm a corporate executive, and I just don't have any time to devote to working out."

I do sympathize—but I don't agree. I remember how things were for me when my first book was published. I was faced with going on a month-long promotional tour while still having to spend every spare moment in my office taking care of other pressing business interests. Usually I had no time to get near a gym. And even when I did, there was so much going on in my mind that I had trouble concentrating. I would be trying to do a Bench Press and suddenly find myself thinking about closing a deal or some other business problem. The distractions had a way of becoming more important than the training.

So I had to learn and adapt. I developed new methods of training, and new attitudes toward my workouts so that I could stay fit and yet take care of business. And it is these methods and attitudes that form the basis of the program you will find in this book. If they work for me, I am certain that they will work for you as well.

The Art of Improvisation

Let me give you an example of what I mean. . . .

I had to go to New York on business recently, so I scheduled a 6 P.M. workout at the Mid-City Gym. But just as I started training, I received a call to come in for an emergency meeting to discuss an upcoming promotional tour.

The meeting was extended, and turned into dinner. By the time I got back to my hotel it was after 11 P.M. I had not had a workout all day, and it was late—so I could have just turned on the television, written a few letters or simply gone to bed. But I didn't. Acting on my own rule that I must do some kind of training every day, I decided to make up for my missed workout.

First I did ten minutes of stretching to loosen up every joint and muscle in my body. Then Leg Raises and Sit-ups for the abdomen, Push-ups for the chest and arms, Handstand Push-ups for the shoulders and some Knee Bends and Lunges for the legs. All of this took only 20 minutes, but I wasn't finished yet.

Cardiovascular training—pumping blood through the circulatory system and air through the lungs—is a very important part of my training. Usually I run to increase my aerobic conditioning, but it was late, and the streets were slippery with snow and ice. So, instead, I went out into the hall, found the service stairs, and quickly ran up ten flights and back down again. Believe me, this gives you a tremendous cardiovascular workout. I came back out of breath, feeling great, took a shower and slept like a baby.

And Now It's Your Turn

Progressive resistance training—working with weights—still forms the basis of my own workouts, and you will find a lot about training with weights in the following pages. But you will also find a lot about flexibility and cardiovascular training, because they are also necessary if you want to really be fit and healthy.

But I also hope to give you some idea of improvisation, the art of getting in a workout of some sort no matter how pressing the demands of time and no matter how far away you are from home and your regular exercise equipment.

In the best of all possible worlds, we would all have plenty of time and energy to devote to keeping fit. But that doesn't happen to be the world I live in —and I don't think it's yours, either. But take heart. Staying in shape no matter how busy you get is possible, and I can show you how this is accomplished. Really.

PART I:
FITNESS AND BODYBUILDING
What Is Fitness?

Physical fitness involves the development of all of the body's physical capabilities.

For example, when exercise physiologists tested weightlifters and bodybuilders about twenty years ago they found these men had tremendous strength and muscular development, but that most of them lacked the endurance that comes from cardiovascular training. Their muscles were in great shape, but not their heart and lungs.

Lifting weights, it was then decided, leads to an unbalanced physical development. But then it occurred to somebody that that kind of a stardard should work both ways. If you test a long-distance runner, you will generally find he has enormous capacity for endurance but, unless he has done some kind of resistance training, he will tend to lack strength, especially in the upper body. He is also unbalanced.

But things have changed a lot since that time. It is now difficult to find a weightlifter or bodybuilder who doesn't do some kind of aerobic training, and many endurance athletes—particularly swimmers—include a lot of strength-training in their workouts. And it is working: the totally fit athlete is not only healthier, but he has an edge over his competitors as well.

I have always followed this principle in my own training. Having been a competitive swimmer and soccer player before I became a bodybuilder, I knew what being in shape really means. So I always included a lot of running and stretching movements in my workouts along with progressive-resistance weight training.

Total fitness, as I see it, has three components:

(1) *Aerobic conditioning.* Aerobic activity is anything that uses up a lot of oxygen. Oxygen is delivered to the muscles by the cardiovascular system —the lungs, heart and circulation of the blood. This system is developed by continuous, high-repetition exercise such as running, swimming, jumping rope, riding a bicycle, etc.

(2) *Flexibility.* Muscles, tendons and ligaments tend to shorten over a period of time, which limits our range of motion and renders us more liable to injury when sudden stresses are placed on these structures. But we can counteract this tendency by stretching exercises and physical programs such as yoga.

(3) *Muscular Conditioning.* There is only one way to develop and strengthen the muscles: resistance training. When you contract the muscles against resistance, they adapt to this level of effort. The best and most efficient way of doing this is through weight training.

Beyond this, once we have the body in shape, we have to learn to use it. This is where sports and athletic activities come in. But we cannot fully enjoy the act of physical play if we haven't developed the basic physical systems with which we have been endowed.

Nutrition and diet are also essential. It makes no sense to make demands on the body if you haven't given it the nutrients it needs to function properly. Therefore an important part of this program involves learning how and what to eat to maximize health and energy.

But of all these areas the one which is most often misunderstood—and which in many ways incorporates the widest range of benefits—is weight training. And the reason that progressive-resistance weight training is so valuable to building and maintaining health and strength become obvious once you take a look at the nature of the muscle that makes up the human body.

The Nature of Muscle

There are three kinds of muscle in the body, each with its own characteristics.

(1) *Smooth muscle* is found in the walls of internal or visceral organs such as blood vessels and intestines.

(2) *Cardiac muscle* is the tissue that makes up the heart, and it can be strengthened by cardiovascular, high-repetition exercise.

(3) *Skeletal muscle* is the system of long muscles that control the movement of the body. It is this kind of muscle, under voluntary control, that weight training is designed to strengthen and condition.

Muscle has one simple function—it contracts. Nothing else. That is why our bodies are designed with opposing muscles or sets of muscles. When you extend or move a part of the body in one direction, it takes the contraction of an opposing muscle to bring it back.

We have muscles because of gravity. Our planet's gravitational field holds us prisoner, and the purpose of muscle is to overcome this basic force. If we lived on a larger planet with a stronger gravitational field, we would have larger muscles. If evolution had prepared us for life on the moon with its one-sixth earth gravity, our muscular structure would be correspondingly lighter.

Muscle is highly adaptive. It changes according to the demands put upon it. For example, a friend of mine broke his leg skiing and was confined to a hospital bed for several weeks. When the cast finally came off, I could hardly believe how thin and weak the injured leg had become. Kept immobile by the cast, the muscles had shrunk noticeably.

The same sort of thing happened to our astronauts who spent so much time in Skylab. I was discussing physical fitness with some NASA officials recently and they told me that these men practically had to learn to walk all over again after returning from long periods of weightlessness in space. Outside the earth's normal gravitational field, their muscles had become maladapted for moving around the planet.

When you lift a weight, or work against some other sort of resistance, you are, in effect, creating an artificial gravitational field. When I was training to win my Mr. Olympia titles and was lifting enormous weights every day in the gym, it was as if I were living on a giant planet like Jupiter instead of the earth. As a result, my body was forced to adapt to this extra effort and my muscles became stronger and more massive.

Since I train these days as much for flexibility, coordination and endurance as for strength, my physique has changed. But by going back to my former hard training for six months or so, I could build myself back up from 215 to my solid 240-pound competition weight. Other people may not be able to make gains like this—a lot of it is genetic—but the basic principle is the same: use a muscle and it gets bigger and stronger; fail to subject it to sufficient stress and it will get weaker and smaller.

Muscle Size and Strength

The shrinking of a muscle due to underuse is called *atrophy*. The increase in size of muscle when it is subjected to greater amounts of stress is called *hypertrophy*.

Muscle tissue itself is composed of bundles of fibers. These fibers are really tiny, and they are wrapped together and bound in a sheath of tissue for strength. We are each given a certain number of these fibers at birth, and we can't increase them through diet, exercise, or any other means. But we can do a lot to alter their size and strength.

Strength is a matter of several factors:

(1) The number of fibers in a muscle.

(2) The number of fibers that participate in any given muscular contraction.

(3) The strength and thickness of the individual fibers.

When you attempt to contract a muscle, you are actually only using a percentage of the fibers that are theoretically available to you. You use only the number that you need to use.

If you keep trying to work against heavier and heavier amounts of resistance, the body adapts by causing more and more of the muscle fibers to engage in the contraction. This takes some time, and there is obviously a physiological limit to this process. But it remains true that the way you get stronger through resistance training is by forcing the muscles to call on increased numbers of muscle fibers to do the work you are asking of them.

In this way, the body is not like a machine. If you connect a 10-horsepower motor to a 12-horsepower load, it will burn out. But if you demand a 12-horsepower effort from a 10-horsepower body, it becomes a 12-horsepower body.

Other things happen to the muscles when you train and condition them. The fibers become enlarged, the sheath covering the muscles gets tougher and the body creates more capillaries to carry more blood to the area.

Progressive-Resistance Training

Exercises like calisthenics, running or swimming are the fixed-resistance kind. That is, no matter how long you do them, you are always contracting the muscles against the same amount of resistance. You may learn to do the movements for longer periods of time, which means your endurance has improved, but you will not get any stronger no matter how many repetitions you do.

To keep getting stronger, you have to keep increasing the resistance so that the muscles must continue to adapt. This is called progressive-resistance training. This is the principle that is used in weight training and bodybuilding.

Progressive-resistance training is a great equalizer. It never gets easy. You may be lifting 10 pounds and I may be lifting 100 pounds, but as long as we are both working at the limit of our strength, we are essentially doing an equal amount of work. All that counts is that we are forcing the muscle to work hard enough to make it adapt.

What Is Bodybuilding?

Although bodybuilders lift weights in order to achieve their physical goals, bodybuilding is not an activity in which the absolute amount of weight you can lift is important. The aim of bodybuilding is to use a sufficient amount of weight for each exercise to cause the adaptive changes in the body that result in the creation of an ideal blend of mass, muscularity, symmetry and proportion.

Weightlifters train with weights, too, but they are only interested in learning to lift as much weight as possible, and then only for the few particular lifts that are involved in competition.

It was long thought that bodybuilders weren't really all that strong, that the mass they developed in the gym was somehow not "real" muscle. This is simply not true. Strength is a necessary by-product of the development of mass and the success of bodybuilders in recent strongman competitions proves it.

But the use of weights in progressive-resistance training is a common denominator among bodybuilders, weightlifers, athletes training for certain sports, individuals with injuries trying to rehabilitate their bodies, and all those millions who are now training for health and fitness.

Weight training, in its most general sense, just means doing some movement or activity using added weight to increase the difficulty. This would include putting weights on your ankles before you run, or swinging a lead-filled bat before your turn at the plate, but usually we restrict the meaning to contracting your muscles in certain, prescribed exercises against the resistance of dumbbells, barbells or resistance exercise machines.

Bodybuilders actually have more in common with the man training for fitness than with competition weightlifters. After all, both are more interested in physical self-improvement than in breaking lifting records.

But there is a large difference in degree. It is as if bodybuilders were Formula I racing cars, and the average man a reliable sports-sedan. Both want a certain degree of performance, but on two distinct levels. The technology that comes out of Grand Prix racing eventually filters down to the family car, and, in the same way, the discoveries made by serious bodybuilders in the gym can be adapted and made use of by those who are using weights to stay trim and healthy.

You may personally have no desire to train for hours a day to become a Mr. America, but exercise physiologists have shown us how much alike in their physical needs are the athlete and the non-athlete. If you apply the techniques that work for champions, only at a level of intensity that suits your own purposes, you will be able to share in the same process that creates, shapes and firms the human body, melts away unwanted fat, and builds a strong, dependable cardiovascular system.

Weight Training—What to Expect

Most men don't really know what to expect from weight training. For instance, it is common in gyms to find some skinny guy just starting training who

assures everybody, "I want to get into better condition, but I don't want to get too big." But, the thing is, getting *really* big is tremendously difficult if not impossible for most people. It takes some eight to twelve years of intense, determined, mind-boggling work to produce a Mr. Olympia physique, and that's only if you have the right genetic potential in the first place. After all, you wouldn't expect necessarily to be able to run a sub-four-minute mile just by practicing a lot. You have to have the talent for it.

But that doesn't mean there is no benefit from weight training for the average man. Quite the contrary. For all but a few there is a definite increase in strength and muscular size along with an improvement in shape and contour of the muscles. The body

gets firmer as muscle fibers become more dense and fat is burned off. The body becomes strong, hard and lean instead of weak, soft and fat.

Some people will change a lot, and others somewhat less. But even seemingly small changes can make a dramatic change in your physique. An inch or two extra around the chest coupled with a loss of a couple of inches around the middle will completely transform how you look. You can never step outside your natural somatotype—the actual structure of your body as determined by your genes—but you can accomplish a great deal within those limits.

It is difficult to increase muscle mass by more than 5 pounds a year. If you have already had extra mass at one time, it is a lot easier to get it back than it is to create it in the first place. A really talented athlete might be able to build 10 pounds of muscle mass a year, but that is a lot.

However, if 5 pounds a year doesn't sound like much, think of it this way: 5 pounds a year is 25 pounds in 5 years. That means a 150-pound man could expect to weigh 175 pounds five years from now with hard training and without gaining any fat.

But, remember, even if you don't really want to get any bigger, all you are doing is increasing your strength to its natural optimum and letting the muscles assume whatever mass is natural to them. A certain amount of mass comes with the territory. The chances of its getting out of hand are pretty remote. And there are a lot of bodybuilders who were never able to develop themselves quite enough who can testify to that!

Meanwhile, as your body improves a psychological benefit comes along with it. You feel better because your training gives you more energy. You feel better about yourself as well, and have greater self-confidence. This affects how you act, and how people treat you. You look better, which makes you feel better. And when you feel better, you naturally end up looking better. It's kind of a non-vicious circle, and it works.

On the Other Hand . . .

In my experience, only a handful of people out of any group get interested enough in training to want to go into it more seriously. However, you might be one of that handful. If you are—and you may be and just not know it yet—let me assure you that the exercise programs outlined in this book are fundamental to bodybuilding as well as weight training for conditioning, and that nothing you learn here will be wasted.

In another section, for those who are interested, I will deal in more detail with the differences between conditioning workouts and competition-oriented bodybuilding training. Actually, you might be surprised at how little difference there really is. We are looking basically at a difference of degree, levels of intensity and a reordering of priorities.

But as the journey of a thousand miles starts with a single step, no matter what you are training for or how far you intend to go, building and shaping your body starts with that first time you pick up a dumbbell or barbell and demand of your muscles that they adapt to working against greater resistance than they are accustomed to.

The Uniqueness of Weight Training

If I seem to be saying that of all the types of exercise and physical fitness systems weight training is the best, it's because I think it is.

Resistance training is the *only* way to build up the body, and progressive resistance training is the only way to insure that this progress continues. It is highly efficient, since you end up doing the most you can during any workout, and thus get the maximum benefit in the least possible time.

It is totally individualized training, since your own development acts as a feedback system to regulate the pace of your training. If you get 5 pounds stronger, you add that much weight. If you progress 10 pounds' worth, that's how much resistance you add to keep your muscles working to their utmost.

Weight training can also be used to promote flexibility. Throughout the program I will be stressing that movements should be done using the widest range of motion possible. At full contraction, you are stretching the opposing muscle group and at full extension you are stretching the muscles that are being trained in the exercise. Combining stretching with strength training is the key to developing a really strong, supple body possessing the most aesthetic lines possible.

Finally, weight training can promote cardiovascular fitness. Obviously, if you lift a heavy weight one or two times, you hardly accelerate your body's need for oxygen, and so the heart and lungs don't get a workout. However, if you lift a weight 8 to 10 times, then go on and lift another the same number of times, then another and so on—after a few minutes of this continuous training, you will begin to demand a great

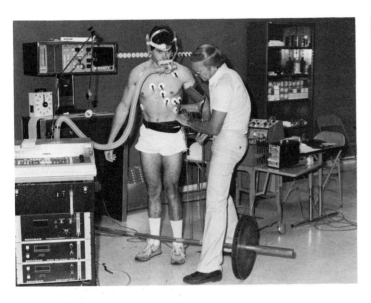

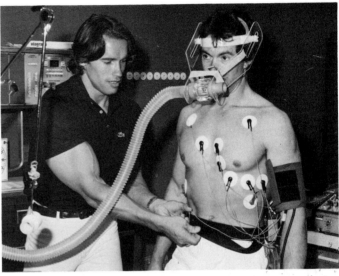

deal from your cardiovascular system. In this way—and this is the kind of exercise program I have designed for you—you combine aerobic training with your strength and flexibility training.

Three-in-one training, that's what you get when you really know how to use weights. And there isn't another training system that can make the same boast.

Weight Training for Health

"About the turn of the century," my friend Dr. Lawrence Golding of the University of Nevada at Las Vegas tells me, "physical educators were telling us that exercise is good for health. But then somebody asked the question, 'Why?' And nobody could really prove why. So they set out to demonstrate this idea that seemed so obvious. That was the birth of what we now know as exercise physiology and sports medicine."

Since then a lot has been learned about exercise and its effects on the body, and I am impressed with the degree that training is important in combating some of the most common physical problems and complaints that plague our population:

(1) *Low back pain.* There are a number of possible causes of back problems—Evolution, which hasn't quite caught up in this area, has given us a back more appropriate to creatures going on all fours—but one of the most common is simply the lack of tone in the back muscles. When the muscles in this area are strong, conditioned and flexible, they do a much better job of supporting the vertebrae and keeping them in their proper place and thus eliminating a number of low back complications.

(2) *Headaches.* Some headaches, perhaps a great proportion, are due to stress. Tension accumulates in the neck and shoulders, blood vessels are constricted. Eventually, pain results. In quite a number of cases, the physical release of exercise can help to alleviate this build-up of stress and do a lot to prevent tension-related headaches.

(3) *Heart disease.* There are a number of forms of heart disease, and many seem to be genetically induced or related to other variables difficult to control. But there is a lot of evidence that exercise, with its effect on the heart and circulatory system, can lower the risk of cardiac problems.

(4) *Pulled muscles.* There is nothing more annoying than reaching up to the top shelf in the kitchen, or going out to the back yard to throw a ball around, and suddenly finding yourself suffering the pain of a strain, sprain or muscle pull. Many of these injuries, however minor, come about simply because the body has been allowed to degenerate somewhat from lack of use. When you are in better condition, when the muscles are firm and strong, the joints, ligaments and tendons flexible, there is much less chance that you will incur this type of injury.

(5) *Insomnia.* Of the many possible causes of insomnia, one, I believe, is living the kind of life where you build up tension through mental effort all day long, but get no physical release through a comparable effort of the body. Man was not meant to just sit around and think and worry. Exercise has a definite effect on the human psychology and can often help solve or reduce a number of mind-related problems.

(6) *Obesity.* It is almost always true that fat people exercise less than thin ones do. Exercise not only burns up more calories in the body, but it seems to have some sort of effect on the appetite-regulation mechanism, an effect that has been observed but never explained. But the simple fact is that exercise is very helpful in controlling weight.

Weight Training and High Blood Pressure

Many people have reservations about training with weights because they have been told it causes high blood pressure. A look at human physiology should be enough to disprove this once and for all.

To start with, just what is "blood pressure?" The human circulatory system consists of a pump (the heart) forcing fluid through a series of pipes (arteries and veins). It takes pressure to make this fluid flow, just as it does to make water flow out of the tap in your kitchen. Our blood pressure is a measure of this pressure.

The heart is a pulsating pump, so we have two blood pressures—the *systolic* when it is pumping, and the *diastolic* when it is not. Whenever you exercise, your heart beats faster and the pressure goes up. If it doesn't you are in trouble. The terminal blood pressure of a top athlete might be 230/110, but his heart and arteries are in condition to take this pressure. If you have been leading a sedentary life and you go out and suddenly try to shovel three feet of snow off your driveway, when your blood pressure suddenly shoots up it could be disastrous.

But exercise and conditioning keep the heart and arteries in shape to deal with the increased pressure. The heavier pulsations of blood shooting through the arteries during exercise actually massage their walls and keep them flexible—helping to prevent hardening of the arteries.

If you already have high blood pressure, obviously you don't want to put sudden strains on the system. Your doctor will no doubt prescribe some mild, rhythmic exercise as part of your therapy. In that case, stressful weight training would not be a good idea.

But in the absence of such symptoms, moderate amounts of weight training, geared progressively to your level of conditioning, will result in only the normal elevation of pressure that comes with any athletic endeavor.

And you get a fringe benefit. Since exercise strengthens the heart and increases its pumping efficiency, as well as keeping the arteries flexible, you will generally find that the conditioned body has a lower blood pressure at rest than the out-of-shape body.

Weight Training and Rehabilitation

Paradoxically, although weight training is designed to put heavy stresses on the muscles of the body, it is being used increasingly to rebuild and rehabilitate injuries.

There are several reasons for this.

(1) With weight training, the precise amount of resistance put on each part of the body can be carefully regulated. Thus a recovering joint or limb can be exercised to promote strength and flexibility without putting any more stress on the area than it can take.

(2) With weight training, stress can be directed at precise and specific areas of the body. Thus you can work around an injury and train strong areas hard, weak areas lightly.

(3) Weight training allows for the development of individually tailored programs. Injuries to the knee, the elbow or a severe muscle tear all require different therapies, and there are such a variety of possible weight training movements that an orthopedist or physiotherapist has plenty to choose from in those cases where resistance training is indicated as a part of the therapy.

Weight Training—the Time Machine

There is one aspect of weight training that is only just coming to be recognized—its effect on the aging process.

The longer we live, the more gravity pulls on our bodies, causing the spine to compress and the muscles to sag. We burn fewer calories as we get older, so we tend to put on fat, and this puts more of a strain on the system. Older people are generally more sedentary than younger ones, and this results in poor cardiovascular conditioning and muscular atrophy.

But a lot of what we think of as "aging" has nothing to do with age itself—it is merely deterioration. When we say somebody "looks" thirty, forty, or fifty, we are merely saying that this person looks the way we *expect* somebody of that age to look. But if you take a look at some older bodybuilders, you will not find any double chins, sagging jowls and pectorals or spreading paunch. Those who have kept up their training—like Bill Pearl or Ed Corney, for example —simply don't fit any of our preconceptions. It is difficult for anyone to judge just how old they are.

Weight training slows or even reverses some of the most insidious effects of age. And it is better at this than any other form of exercise. I had a physical recently and my doctor was amazed at my condition. He told me that I was in as good or better health than I was ten years ago. And all because I have kept up my training.

Judging on the basis of blood pressure, cholesterol level, flexibility and heart rate, I have actually gotten physiologically younger during the past ten years instead of older. And this is a direct result of the kind of training and diet that I am advocating in this book.

Age is bound to catch up with all of us sooner or later. But later is better. No need to invite it in before its time. So when people ask me if they are too old to train, I tell them, "No. You're too old not to!"

The older you are, the more important it is for you to work at being physically fit. But it is also true that the older you are, the more amazed you will be at what a total fitness program, including weight training, can do for you, your life, your looks, your health and your personal relationships.

Winning at Life

Now we know you must develop both your mind and body, that it is truly unhealthy to ignore either one.

It is an outdated cliché to think in categories of "athlete" and "non-athlete" as if these were two different species, one from Mars, the other Venus.

Everything we do throughout our lives has a physical component. We are physical creatures, and life demands that we put our bodies to use—breathing, standing, sitting, lying down, walking, running, lifting, carrying, making love, fighting, singing, throwing, climbing and so on.

Once you realize that life is an athletic event, it follows that you can train for it, just as Bruce Jenner trained for the Olympics or I trained to become a six-time Mr. Olympia winner. You may not train like a competition athlete, but you will need to develop the fitness, strength and conditioning that it takes for you to excel at your own personal event—in this case, your life.

Our bodies and our minds are totally interrelated and interdependent. In sports, a running back who tires in the fourth quarter is taken from the game. A fighter too tired to answer the bell for the tenth round loses the bout. But in the event of life, you don't get another chance next Sunday afternoon and you can't sign for a rematch. Once you get taken out of this game, that's it, brother. No second chances. And if that's not a reason to stay in shape, I don't know what is!

No Cynics Need Apply

Still, it is very difficult sometimes to convince people of the necessity for exercising to stay fit. We are able to take our bodies so much for granted because they are so well designed. We can often abuse them for decades before we see the inevitable signs of deterioration. Using the car analogy again, a man who owns a high-performance Ferrari knows he has to take very good care of it or it will not run properly. It has to be taken out and run at high speeds or the plugs foul and carbon builds up on the pistons. The Chevrolet owner, on the other hand, can generally afford to think about maintenance only from time to time, because his machine has been designed for greater durability.

Well, the human body has the performance capability of a Ferrari, and the durability of the Chevy. Although we need to put ourselves through the human equivalent of an all-out lap at Le Mans from time to time, we can also idle along for thirty years before we starting having serious maintenance problems. No machine was ever designed to compare with this combination of performance and durability.

The Art of Motivation

Getting in shape, building and conditioning your body for strength and health, is no great problem if you know the proper techniques—and you will find those techniques outlined in this book.

The real problem is applying what you know, getting yourself to practice what I am preaching, so to speak. Because I can tell you that you ought to get yourself into shape, your doctor can advise you that it is good for your health and your wife or girl friend can hint that she would be more turned on if you shaped up a bit—but none of this is going to make the slightest difference until you, yourself, decide that this is really what you want to do.

The first step is simply believing it is possible. A lot of people never achieve this. They are so used to themselves as they have been, looking and feeling a

certain way, that they cannot imagine any dramatic change. "Hey, I'm a naturally skinny (fat) type," they say. "It's in my genes. My whole family is like this. There's nothing I can do about it."

To a certain degree, this is correct. None of us can step outside the boundaries of our genetic inheritance. But within those limits there is a tremendous amount we can do to manipulate our physical systems, gain muscle and lose fat, and realize the full genetic potential that nature has given to us.

You can't make yourself taller or alter your basic skeletal structure, but you can firm and shape the body, fill out skinny areas, shape muscles and create the kind of firm, healthy body you would really rather have.

Visualization

But to keep yourself motivated, you are going to have to train the mind along with the body. Using your mind and your imagination properly you can keep the body training intensely throughout your workouts.

One technique to help you with this is called "visualization." It is the art of picturing in your mind the results you would like to see happen, and using these images to focus all your energies on attaining your goals.

A psychologist friend of mine has told me that one reason he believes I was so successful was my ability at visualization. "Arnold," he said, "in your imagination you always saw yourself as the champion, the victor. The others imagined how terrible it would be to lose and their fears kept them from doing their best. But with your positive attitude, you always had the confidence it took to win."

I understood the concept of visualization long before I had ever heard the word. From the first day of my training, I realized that my competition understood exercise, diet and nutrition, and that the way people really differed was mentally and psychologically. What counts is really believing in yourself and what you want, and I became a master of this. When you hear about ideas like "Inner Tennis" or "Inner Skiing," this is what they are talking about. And the same techniques can be applied to your weight training.

You can do this, too. Look in the mirror and take stock of what you see. Be honest and admit your faults, but, at the same time, imagine what you would look like if those faults were corrected. Picture yourself with a deeper chest, broader shoulders and a smaller, tighter waistline.

Once you know what your goals are, your training efforts make more sense. After all, you wouldn't get on a train or plane without knowing its destination —and you shouldn't do this with your workouts, either. Keep that image of the future firmly in mind, and your imagination will help you to make it a reality.

Exercise and the Spirit

Exercise and conditioning have a profound effect on the mind and spirit as well as on the body. Modern life puts all of us under a tremendous amount of stress which engages our "fight or flee" emergency nervous system, floods our bodies with adrenaline—

but gives us no outlet for all that pent-up energy.

A caveman faced with a saber-tooth tiger or a woolly mammoth would hardly be expected to smile politely and swallow his anger, but that is what most of us have to do when aroused by stressful situations in our business and social lives.

Nature simply won't allow us to suffer that kind of abuse without paying some kind of penalty. Nature just hasn't gotten around to recognizing the Industrial Revolution, self-cleaning ovens, the internal combustion engine or the desk job. Biologically, we are still cavemen, equipped to survive by using both body and mind. We need to engage in a full range of physical activities, just as our bodies need a full range of foods for adequate nutrition.

Training gives us an outlet for suppressed energies created by stress and thus tones the spirit just as exercise conditions the body. We all know how stress can contribute to such physical ailments as ulcers, high blood pressure and hypertension. But it is also becoming clear that a lot of human problems from auto accidents to divorces, and many common emotional problems like depression, are made much worse by the build-up of stress accompanied by too little physical activity.

The New Consensus

Ten years ago, if I had made some of these claims, I might have gotten an argument. But not any more. Actuarial figures gathered by insurance companies bear out the benefits of physical conditioning to health, mood and lifespan. And the major corporations are beginning to catch on, too. Some organizations, like Warner Communications in New York, are opening up sophisticated gyms and training facilities for their employees. In fact, there are over 50 businesses in New York City alone which have similar programs, and more catching on all the time all across the country.

A business often spends as much on training good executives and other personnel as it does on building factories and offices, and this kind of investment calls for protection. When an employee breaks down or gets sick, it can hurt the business financially just as badly as a breakdown in the factory or on the assembly line. It has been shown that an employee who is fit and healthy works better, more efficiently, with less time off the job due to sickness and less chance that his employer will lose his services prematurely due to problems like heart disease and stroke.

Physical fitness is a form of preventive maintenance. I know I could never survive my own schedule without devoting time to staying fit. And I am not alone in this, either. Almost all the really effective executives and businessmen that I know have also come to this realization. No longer is it solely the province of the young and the professional to have superb bodies and be superbly fit.

Physical fitness is not a panacea. It won't, by itself, do away with anxiety, drug and alcohol abuse, sexual dysfunction and all the rest of the common physical and emotional problems of modern society.

But an ill-used body will ultimately result in the failure of both body and spirit, and, in this sense, physical fitness is the mental health of the body. We live in a culture that has taken away the need to use physical strength for day-to-day survival, so it is up to us to create new systems of living that provide the level of fitness that the body requires.

For one thing, there is simply the joy of being able to use your body to get the pleasures of strenuous play. What a difference between being able to play a game of touch football, go sailing or skiing and really have a good time—and being soft, flabby and cut off from your natural abilities. I've seen people sitting around the pool or on the beach who are obviously out of place and ill at ease simply because they have let their bodies and physical capabilities degenerate. I know how unhappy I would be if this happened to me, and I can't believe that other people are all that different.

This is where a program of physical training such as the one in this book comes in. Weight training, aerobic conditioning and flexibility are the bottom-line demands of any fitness system. Try it, and I know you will get the results that you really want.

Good luck, and good training!

Getting Started

First Things First

There is nothing like the enthusiasm we all feel when we get into new beginnings—a new job, relationship, or even a new health and fitness program. Therapists call this the "honeymoon period," and it's just common sense to realize that this initial enthusiasm doesn't last.

I can't tell you the number of times I've seen newcomers come into the gym and attack every piece of equipment in sight as if they were training for the Olympics—only to end up painfully sore and discouraged.

But that isn't going to happen to you. I can show you how to develop your body, increase your strength and improve your energy level, and then it is up to you to pace yourself in a realistic manner.

Are you 20, 30 or over 40? Have you been active and athletic in the last few years, or pretty much sedentary? Maybe you have some long-term physical ailment like a trick knee or a bad back. All of these things have to be taken into consideration as you begin my exercise program.

Just as in the story of the tortoise and the hare, slow and steady wins the fitness race, too. So remember you are only training yourself. You have nobody else to please. Be honest, set yourself realistic goals and training schedules, and you'll find the results worth all the effort.

Begin with a Check-up

Consult your doctor before beginning any new kind of strenuous physical activity. Not only can your doctor advise you on any special adjustments you might have to make in following a fitness program, but he can periodically monitor your progress, giving you additional positive feedback to keep your motivation level high.

Definition of Terms

You can't build up your body with words, but it helps communication if you can understand the special terminology of weight training and bodybuilding. You'll find a complete glossary at the end of this book, but here are a few basic terms to help you get started:

A *Repetition* ("rep" for short) is one complete exercise movement, from starting position, through the full range of movement, then back to the beginning.

A *Set* is a group of repetitions. The number is arbitrary. It could be one, or 100. Programs designed to produce cardiovascular fitness generally use high-repetition sets, while those that aim for strength use fewer repetitions.

A *Superset* is a set of one exercise followed by a set of another with zero rest in between.

A *Circuit* is a prescribed group of exercises. Circuit training involves going through this group one after another without stopping to rest between exercises.

Weight training is done with weights. Actually, anything that provides adequate resistance can be used for training purposes, but weights are simple, efficient and convenient to use. The two basic forms in use today are free weights, and exercise machines.

Free weights include:

The *Barbell,* a long bar with weights at either end,

designed to be used by both hands at once.

The *Dumbbell*, a short bar with weights at either end, intended for use by one hand at a time.

Exercise machines are mechanical devices that allow you to contract your muscles against resistance. These can include everything from the simple push-pull devices you can carry in a suitcase, to weight-and-pulley set-ups, to the complex and highly engineered training devices manufactured by such companies as Nautilus and Universal.

In this program, we will rely primarily on free weights, using some mechanical help only for specialized purposes. Later on, as you become a more experienced weight-trainer, you will have the option of employing other devices if you wish.

Muscles and Body Parts

Bodybuilders have found over the years that it is useful to think of the muscles and muscle groups in the body as falling into certain basic categories. The five basic categories are:

legs	chest
back	arms
shoulders	

with calves & abdominals considered separately—for reasons I will explain later on in the program.

There are more than 600 muscles in the body, so grouping them together this way provides a convenient way of dealing with them. However, it is a good idea to know the names of certain of the most important muscles so that when I talk about "biceps," "deltoids" or "trapezius" you will know which ones I mean. The names of the more significant muscles and muscle groups are shown in the accompanying illustration.

Weight training routines are designed so that each body part receives adequate attention. But, more than that, it is frequently necessary to use a variety of different exercises for one muscle or muscle group to bring out all the planes, shape and contour of the body, so planning a really good routine can be a challenging, demanding and technical discipline.

Keeping Score

As your body changes, you will want to be able to keep careful track of differences of fat, muscle and strength. Keeping track provides a very useful form of positive feedback, as well as letting you know if any problems are developing. There are several ways of going about this:

● *The Scale.* Body weight is made up of several factors.

(**1**) The fixed weight of the body, including the skeleton, internal organs and vital fluids such as blood.

(**2**) The weight of fat.

(**3**) The weight of muscle.

The first factor can't be varied to any great degree by diet and exercise, but the others can. However, while the scale may accurately record your body weight at any one time, it says nothing about body composition.

The average man in this country has about 15% relative body fat. A good athlete can have as little as 2%–3%. With an intense program of weight training,

WRIST

FOREARM

DELTOID

TRAPEZIUS

BICEPS

PECTORALS

ABDOMINALS

QUADRICEPS

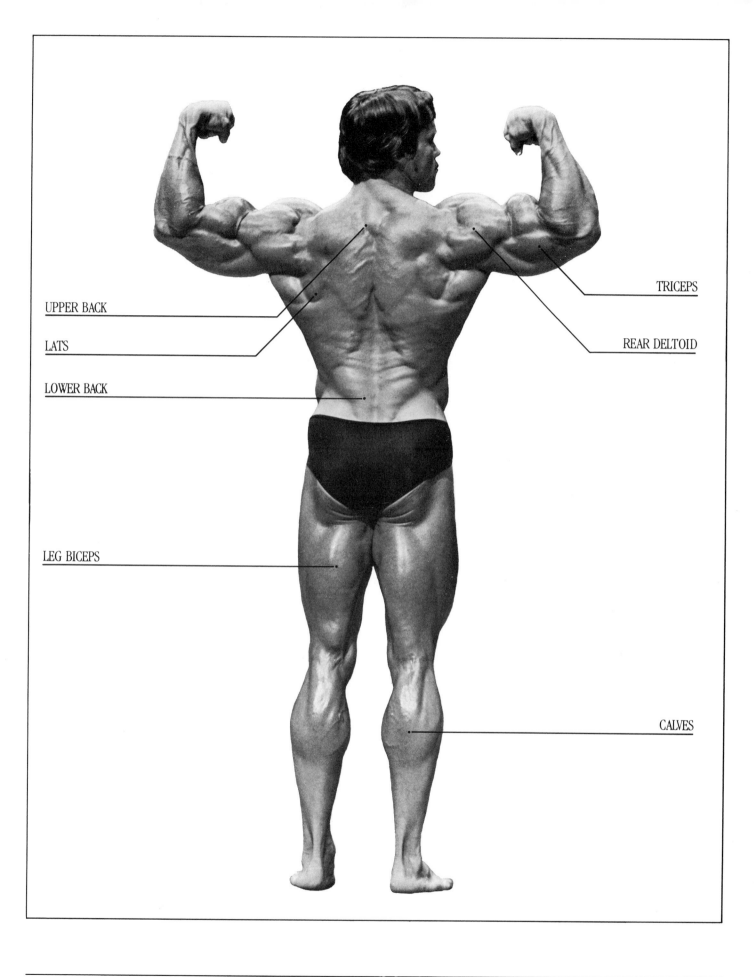

UPPER BACK

LATS

LOWER BACK

LEG BICEPS

TRICEPS

REAR DELTOID

CALVES

individuals can gain from 5 to 15 pounds of muscle weight a year. Losing 5 pounds of fat while gaining 5 pounds of muscle can change your body radically. The scale will not be able to measure this change. You will see it and feel it.

Then there is "water weight." Contrary to what many people believe, the free water in your system gets flushed out within a relatively short time of its ingestion. But water is retained in other ways. For instance, whenever the body stores a gram of glycogen (carbohydrate energy) it binds three grams of water in the process. Furthermore, when the body metabolizes a gram of fat, more than a gram of water accumulates as a byproduct of this process and it takes a while for this water to leave the system.

Considering all of these variables, it becomes obvious that simply knowing how much you weigh doesn't really tell you enough about what is happening to the body. The scale has to be used judiciously, and I recommend two simple rules:

(1) *Don't weigh yourself too often.* You can't get an accurate picture of real changes in body weight on a day-to-day basis. So weigh yourself no more often than once a week.

(2) *Don't rely on the scale alone.* Use it in conjunction with the tape-measure, the mirror and before-and-after photos.

● *The Tape Measure.* Measuring various parts of the body can tell you things about its composition and development that the scale alone cannot. Therefore, as you begin this program, measure yourself and note down the results for the following areas:

neck	——
upper arm	——
chest	——
waist	——
thigh	——
calf	——
forearm	——

This will give you a good basis of comparison for following your progress.

However, just as with the scale, don't take comparison measurements too often. The only place where the tape measure is likely to show changes week-to-week is around the waistline. You can lose fat around the middle faster than you can gain muscle size, although that result will follow soon enough.

Actually, very small changes in muscle mass can have highly dramatic results in the way you look. A gain of two inches around the chest coupled with a loss of another two around the waist can give your body a totally different appearance. People begin to notice these changes very quickly, and no other sport or system of physical training makes such a difference in how you look so quickly. So when it comes to assessing just how well you are doing in your training, it is often a better idea to rely on the mirror instead of the tape measure.

● *The Mirror.* The mirror has a number of different uses for bodybuilders and weight trainers (see next chapter), but its basic purpose is to tell you how you look. Studying yourself in a full-length mirror can be misleading if you let your imagination take the place of honest evaluation. Unlike visualization, all you want from a mirror is so see things the way they are, here and now. Use the mirror to gauge your progress, to see where you have made gains, and to pinpoint areas that are in need of more work.

● *Before-and-After Photos.* We all have a way of failing to notice small gradual changes, but photographs can quickly remind us just how great the overall change has been.

Have some photos taken of yourself in a bathing suit from the front, rear and sides. Then put them away for a while, along with a record of your weight and measurements at the time the photos were taken.

When you think you've made some progress, repeat the process, and compare the "before" photos with the "after." You may be very surprised at the differences that become apparent when you study the two sets of pictures.

Continue to do this. The photographs will not only help you evaluate the results of your training during each of the intervals, but will also create a permanent history of the changes in your body as a result of your weight training program. You will probably discover you are smiling a lot more.

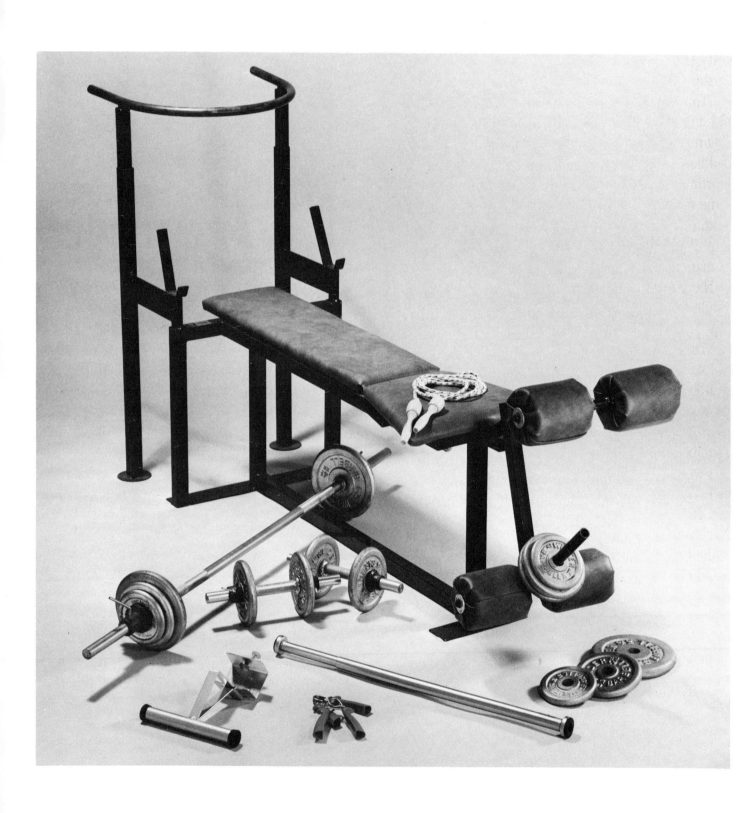

Belly Up To The Barbell

To start with you will need a barbell and dumbbell set. This consists of a long bar, two shorter ones, and a number of weight plates that fit interchangeably on any of the bars. You can find a basic set with 50 kilos or 110 pounds of weights in almost any sporting goods store for as little as forty dollars. Some of these sets have plastic plates filled with sand, others are made of iron. Either kind is suitable. Plastic has the advantage that it won't scratch or mar a floor.

There are only two necessities in choosing a weight set:

(1) The weights must be interchangeable. Progressive resistance training demands that you be able to add weight to the bar as you get stronger. Solid dumbbells, to which weight cannot be added, won't allow you to take advantage of the adaptation of muscle to progressively greater stress. If you do get solid dumbbells, you will need an entire set—and that gets expensive.

(2) The set must include 2½-pound plates. Some sets come with no plates smaller than 5 pounds. Since you add weight by putting a plate on either end of the bar, this means that the smallest addition you could make would be 10 pounds, and this is just too much of a jump for most people in many of the exercises. 2½-pound plates allow for more convenient 5-pound weight adjustments.

In addition to the weights, you are going to need an exercise bench. The basic bench looks a lot like a piano bench, but is padded to allow for comfort during physical movement. However, without a somewhat more sophisticated bench, certain basic exercises cannot be done in the home. So I recommend that you purchase a bench with a rack that allows you to do Bench Presses, and an attachment under which you hook your legs to do Leg Extensions and Leg Curls.

These benches can be very expensive but can also be had for less than a hundred dollars. Just be sure yours is sturdy enough to stand up to your needs.

Another basic piece of equipment is the chinning bar. Without using fairly complex exercise machines, the chinning bar is one of the only ways of developing certain areas of the back. Adjustable bars that fit into most doorways are also available at most sporting goods stores.

I also recommend that you get a slant board to help you do Sit-ups for firming up the waistline and abdominal muscles. But be careful to try out whatever board you purchase before you take it home. Some of them are very flimsy. There is a lot of difference between having a 105-pound woman use a device and subjecting it to the forces generated by an active 190-pound man.

You may also run across a device that slides under a door and provides support for your feet when you do Sit-ups. These are good because they are small enough to take with you when you travel, so you can continue to train your abdominal muscles even when you are staying in a hotel.

What Not to Use

There are a lot of manufacturers trying to cash in on the national craze for exercise and fitness with devices and springs and levers and chrome doodads that are supposed to help you get in shape. For anyone really serious about training, these things are a waste of money.

Exercise, any kind of exercise, is generally better than no exercise at all. Walking is better for you than sitting in front of a television set and playing a sport is better for your health than just being a spectator.

But pulling, pushing or twisting some kind of mechanical contraption is no substitute for a well thought-out, carefully designed system of physical fitness.

A complete weight-training program allows you to work the whole body, not just a few muscles or muscle groups. Fooling around with some "miracle device" does not.

Later on, when we talk about Improvisational Exercise, I will recommend some substitutes for weight training to be used when weights are not available. But when it comes to getting the full benefits of progressive-resistance training, there is nothing like the real thing.

The Home Gym

There are some good "home gyms" on the market, some much more expensive than others, for those who want to train at home with more sophisticated equipment than just some free weights and a bench. A complete Universal machine can easily run into the thousands of dollars, although there are some less complicated but useful devices that cost less than $600.00.

For most people who want to go beyond the limitations of home training with simple equipment, I would recommend joining a gym or health club. However, if you can handle the expense, having good sophisticated equipment available to you at home is a very convenient and pleasant way to train.

The Mirror

The mirror is a valuable tool for anyone taking up weight training.

1. *It helps concentration.* A big part of weight training is getting the nervous system to fire off as many muscle fibers as possible. Concentration is a major factor in making this happen. Using the mirror to focus attention is indispensible to the serious weight trainer.

2. *It helps technique.* When you train with weights, you don't just throw them around. There is a definite technique involved which allows you to work each muscle the way you want and prevents any undue stress on the body from lack of control over the weight. Watching yourself in the mirror lets you correct any deviations from proper technique—just as it does in a discipline like ballet.

3. *It provides feedback.* The name of the game, after all, is to change the body. Part of that change is recognized by feel; the rest is visual. If looking in the mirror and seeing a new curve in the biceps, a fullness in the chest, keeps you dedicated and working hard, then that's fine. Success breeds success. It's the same in weight training as in any other area of life.

Where to Train

If you have access to a gym you can train there, following this program, right from day one. But if you don't and you want to train at home, all you need is the basic equipment and enough room so you don't put the end of a barbell through the front of your television set.

Enough room is important. You may need more than you think. Even if you have enough clearance to work with the weights, if it feels as though you may not and you are continually distracted by the possibility of banging into something, this can seriously interfere with your concentration. You might try training in the living room, bedroom or den, out in the garage or even the back yard, wherever you find it most convenient.

A few other things you might want include a certain degree of privacy—family members parading through the room can also break your concentration —enough light to see well, and a good amount of air circulation.

When to Eat
When our mothers told us not to go in the water right after eating, what they meant (whether they knew it or not) was that digestion takes blood, and so does heavy exercise. Therefore, in order to have enough blood available to feed your muscles, you want to avoid doing any strenuous exercise while your stomach is full.

Protein and fat take a long time to digest, so you might want to wait quite a while after eating a steak before you train. Salads and vegetables take less time to pass through the stomach, so you needn't wait as long. Fruit digests very quickly, and the fructose (sugar) it contains converts easily to glucose to provide energy for exercise, so you can eat moderate amounts of fruit just before and even during your workout.

Do It to Music
I am often asked in my seminars, "Does it help to have music in the background when you train?" The answer is simply that it helps if you think it helps. If you like training to music, then go ahead and do it. But use common sense: you will hardly be able to keep your energy level up listening to Strauss waltzes. Pick something that adds to your workout, not something that puts you to sleep.

When to Train
Picking a time to train that fits conveniently into your daily schedule is important. I like to get up and go to the gym or run by 6:30 in the morning. By nine or ten I have trained, showered, eaten breakfast and am ready to face the day's business.

But some people can hardly bring themselves to shave first thing in the morning, much less do a workout. If that's the case then, you might find it better to train after you get home from work and before dinner. It wouldn't hurt to skip that cocktail, either.

I meet a number of men who have access to gyms during their lunch hour and prefer to do their training then, and skip eating. Again, that's a matter of personal choice and circumstances.

There is a special form of training called the "Split System" that involves training part of your body in the morning and additional body parts later in the day. This is useful for those who don't really have one long period to devote to training but still want to get in a full workout. I describe how to train with the Split System later on in the advanced exercise section.

Missing Workouts

A lot of things can happen to interfere with a scheduled workout. When that happens there is no use in getting upset about it. The trick is to do *something* every day, even if it only involves taking a walk or doing some sit-ups and calisthenics. For those times when you are away from home and can't follow your regular weight-training routine, I have included some substitute exercises that I use later on in the "Improvisational Training" section of this book.

Overcoming Inertia

The longest journey begins with the first step. This is as true with weight training as anything else. The only way to get started is to start, but this involves making changes in your life.

Making these changes can be difficult. We are used to living our lives in familiar, convenient patterns and it's tough to change. Beyond that, friends, family and co-workers often do not understand what it is you are trying to do, and getting their cooperation can be difficult.

Everyone is out to steal your time, and you have to be selfish about your training. From morning to night, other people make demands on your attention, and you just have to resist letting them take that 45 minutes you need for training. Sometimes they may even be resentful or jealous because you are doing something they cannot. But once they get used to the "new you," if they really care about you, they will accept it, and even forget that things were ever any different.

So get your equipment, find a place and the time to train, and get going. Jump right in—believe me, the water's fine!

PART II
THE PROGRAM

Getting Ready

You should never subject your body and your muscles to any sudden strain for which they are not prepared. The stronger you get, the better your condition, the truer this is. Think about it—the more power you are able to generate, the more stress you can put on the muscle-tendon-joint-ligament network. Therefore, you never get in such good shape that you don't need to warm up before you train. And this warm-up should consist of two parts:

Stretching, to lengthen your muscles, tendons and ligaments as much as possible to produce maximum flexibility;

High-repetition, aerobic exercise to get the heart and lungs working and to increase the blood supply to the muscles.

The Three-Part Approach

The program I have designed for you, which is virtually identical to the one I follow myself, actually consists of one additional element . . . *warming down.*

I could call this *cooling down,* but that makes it sound as if it is not really part of the exercise program, just a kind of tail following the dog around. This is not true. I believe that a program of careful stretching, following the vigorous contractions of a weight-training program, does a great deal toward making you feel better, increasing overall flexibility and really setting you up for the rest of the day.

Warming down is one of the most pleasant parts of physical training. You give yourself time for your blood pressure to come down, for your heart to slow to its normal rate and you end up feeling calm, relaxed and really good.

Why Flexibility?

Physical fitness experts stress that being loose, stretching your muscles and joints is good for you, but they seldom say why. Of course, the fact that being flexible prevents the kind of injury that occurs when a muscle-tendon-joint structure is overstretched is not hard to understand. But there are other reasons.

One of them involves tension. Physical and mental tension are closely related. Psychological stress tends to build up tension in the muscles, which prolongs and encourages emotional tension. Remember what a tremendous feeling of relief it was the last time someone came up and massaged your neck and shoulders after you sat working hunched over a desk? Most of us get so used to being tense that we forget about it—but it hurts us anyway.

Then there is energy. When you have a wheel turning on an axle that needs to be greased, think of how much more energy it takes to move the vehicle. The body doesn't squeal and squeak like a rusty axle, but tension works just the same to produce drag and wasted energy.

Tense, inflexible muscles and joints waste energy in two ways. On the one hand, keeping various muscles contracted for long periods wastes energy without providing any of the benefits of exercise. On the other, whenever you try to move a part of the body against the resistance of an opposing muscle that is unnecessarily contracted, all you are doing is making the movement more difficult, ungainly and fatiguing. When you are loose and flexible, your movements become smoother and require less energy, and your coordination is vastly improved.

The Three-Level Program

Weight training forms the core of this program, but flexibility training is also very important. Before you start working with the weights each day, I want you to set aside enough time to do the stretching moves without rushing.

Once you have gotten loose and relaxed, then go on to the warm-up movements. These are somewhat more strenuous, and are designed to get your heart and lungs working at full efficiency. When you do these movements you work up a sweat and actually warm up the muscles—raise their temperature— just as you warm up the engine of a car to make it run more efficiently with more power.

The stretching and warm-ups are important, and you should include them in each and every workout. After completing this part of the program, you will be ready to do your weight training and get the most out of it.

But you are not finished yet. After putting away the weights, take a little time to warm down afterward. These movements will counteract any shortening of the muscles, tendons and ligaments that can be induced by weight training.

(Incidentally, weight training doesn't produce the kind of inflexibility many people think it does—but using the contractions of one muscle to stretch the opposing muscle is something that it takes quite a bit of training experience to accomplish.)

Progress in flexibility is measured in fractions of an inch. So don't be in a hurry. Just concentrate on how much better and more relaxed you feel when you have gone through these movements.

Take your time, and don't worry if you can't stretch as far as the people in the illustrations. They are, after all, experts. Just try to stretch a fraction farther with each repetition, each exercise session, and those fractions will sooner or later add up to substantial gains.

1. Neck Rolls

This is a deceptively simple but vital exercise. The neck and shoulders are the repository of a lot of the body's tensions, and Neck Rolls are the first step toward physical relaxation.

The Exercise

Stand upright, hands at your sides. Breathe deeply, letting your shoulders, arms and whole body relax as much as possible. Now slowly let your head fall forward until your chin touches your chest. Feel the stretch in the back of the neck.

Begin to rotate your head and neck to the left, as if trying to touch the left ear to the left shoulder. The movement should be done slowly, feeling the stretch continue in the neck muscles.

Gilad Janklowicz: The decathlon champion from Israel who is still in training for the next Olympics

Continue the rotation around to the back, to the right side, and then all the way around again to the front. Take as much time for this movement as you want. The slower the better.

After one complete rotation to the left, do another one slowly, all the way around to the right.

Repetitions:
5 rolls to each side

Date & Reps	Date & Reps

STRETCHING

2. Side Bends

This movement stretches the
muscles of the lower torso,
particularly those that run
down either side (external
obliques).

The tendency in this exercise, as in many stretching
movements, is to try to get
maximum extension by
"bouncing" and stretching
the body further than it really
wants to go. I recommend
you never do this. Stretch and
hold, but don't bounce. You
can hurt yourself with any
kind of violent movement.

The Exercise
Stand upright, feet very wide
apart. Raise your right hand
high overhead, and put your
left hand down on the side of
your left leg. Stretch upward
with your right arm as high
as you can, and then begin
bending to your left, continuing the stretch, and sliding
your left hand down your left
leg for support.

Bend as far as you can
and reach with your right
hand as if trying to touch the
wall on your left. Hold for a
count of 5, and then
straighten up slowly to the
starting position.

Lower your right arm,
raise your left, and repeat the
Side Bend to your right.

Repetitions:
10 times to each side

3. Lunges/ Achilles Stretches

This is a combination exercise designed to stretch the front of the thighs (quadriceps), the inner thighs, the back of the legs (hamstrings), the calves and the lower back.

The Exercise

Begin with the Lunge. From a standing position with your feet together, step forward as far as you can with the left foot, keeping both feet pointed straight ahead. Bend your left knee and lower yourself as far as you can, keeping your back and your right leg straight. Put your hands down on either side of the forward foot for balance.

This movement is followed by the Achilles Stretch. Push up with your hands and straighten the left leg, but stay bent over with your hands remaining by your left foot. Keep both feet in place and flat on the floor, feeling the stretch in the back of your left leg and the Achilles' tendon of your right. Bend your head down as close as possible to the left knee.

From this position, lower yourself again to the lunging position.

Repetitions:
5 combinations

Date & Reps　　**Date & Reps**

4. Combination Hamstring Stretches

This is another combination exercise designed to stretch the lower back and the back of the legs.

The Exercise

After completing the previous Lunge, come up to the Achilles Stretch position, stand upright and pivot to the right so that your feet are parallel, still wide apart.

Bend forward, keeping your back as straight as possible. This ensures that you stretch the lower part of the back. Touch your hands to the floor directly in front of you and hold this position for a 5-count.

Slowly turn your torso and walk your hands over to your left foot, and take hold of your left ankle. Keep your legs straight, knees locked. Pulling gently with your hands, put your head as close to the left knee as possible. Hold this position for a 5-count.

Let go of your ankle, and slowly walk your hands across your right side and take hold of your right ankle. Gently stretch and hold for a 5-count.

Repetitions:
5 stretches to each side

5. Lunges/ Achilles Stretches

This is the same combination exercise you did earlier, only this time it is done to the other side.

The Exercise

From the Hamstring Stretch, pivot to your right, bend your right knee, and come forward in the Lunge position. Repeat the Lunge/Achilles Stretch movements to this side.

Repetitions:
5 combinations

Date & Reps **Date & Reps**

47

Picking Up the Pace

Now it is time for more vigorous movement. For warming up we use aerobic exercise, which simply means movement that demands the use of a lot of oxygen. Quick, high-repetition exercise gets the lungs working to put more oxygen into the bloodstream, picks up the heart rate so that more blood is pumped to the various muscles, and warms up those muscles to get them ready to contract against heavier resistance.

With all of the following exercises, start out taking it easy until your body gets used to the effort, then pick up the pace.

1. Standing Twists

This movement works the muscles of the torso by twisting them against the resistance of the lower body. In all twisting movements, keep the hips stationary so that they provide the necessary resistance.

The Exercise

Stand with your feet flat on the floor, wide apart, knees slightly bent to keep the hips from turning. Raise your arms out to either side, bend your elbows and hold the arms about chest level, parallel to the floor.

Keeping your head facing forward at all times, twist your shoulders and upper body as far to the right as you can without letting your hips turn. Then twist back as far as you can to the left.

Start out easy, letting the muscles stretch and get used to the effort. As you get warmed up, put more energy into the movement.

Repetitions:
20 to each side

Date & Reps	**Date & Reps**

2. Bent-Over Twists

This is simply the same movement as Standing Twists, but done with your upper body bent over. Although this works the same muscles, by changing the angle you exercise another part of the muscle.

The Exercise

As soon as you finish your repetitions of the Twists, bend over so that your torso is parallel to the floor. Continue the twisting movement, keeping the hips stationary, and try to touch each elbow to the opposite knee.

Repetitions:
20 to each side

3. Windmills

The Exercise

Stay in the bent-over position, straighten your arms out to each side, and twist so that you touch your right hand to your left foot, calf or knee, whichever you can reach. Your left arm should remain straight and end up pointing at the ceiling. At the same time, turn your head so that you are looking up behind you.

Repeat the movement to the other side, touching your left hand to your right leg.

Repetitions:
20 to each side

4. High Knees

	Date & Reps	Date & Reps

This is a running-in-place movement that is very popular with athletes who want to develop greater speed, agility and endurance. Houston McTear, the world's fastest sprinter, sometimes spends entire afternoons doing just this exercise.

The Exercise

From a standing position, begin running in place and try to bring each knee just as high as you possibly can in front of you.

Stay on the balls of your feet throughout this exercise, since landing on your heels can result in injury.

As you go through this exercise, try to speed up a little at a time, and continue to try getting your knees higher and higher.

Repetitions:
20 with each leg

5. Jumping Lunges

If High Knees is running in place, this is a kind of walking in place or lunging in place.

The Exercise
Stand upright with your feet together. Begin the exercise with a slight jump, one foot going forward and the other one back. The front leg is bent, and the rear leg kept straight.

As you do this lunging motion, swing your arms. When your left leg goes forward, swing your right arm forward, left arm back. The opposite arm and leg stay together.

The wider you split your feet apart, and the more you bend your front leg and lower yourself toward the floor, the more difficult the movement.

After your initial lunging jump, give another slight jump and, in one motion, reverse your legs—rear leg coming forward, forward leg coming back. As you switch the positions of your legs, do the same with your arms.

Repetitions:
20 in each position

_____ _____
_____ _____
_____ _____
_____ _____
_____ _____
_____ _____
_____ _____
_____ _____
_____ _____
_____ _____
_____ _____
_____ _____
_____ _____
_____ _____
_____ _____
_____ _____
_____ _____
_____ _____
_____ _____
_____ _____
_____ _____
_____ _____
_____ _____
_____ _____
_____ _____

The Finishing Touch

The following 7 exercises should be done immediately after you have finished your weight training. At this point, when your muscles are pumped and warm, you will find that progress in flexibility comes rapidly.

1. Hamstring Stretches

You will recognize this as the familiar "touch your toes" movement. Remember, as you do the exercise, you want to stretch and hold, not bounce or force your body farther than it can readily go.

The Exercise

Stand with your feet together, legs straight, knees locked. Bend forward from the waist, keeping your back straight. Again, by not bending your back you produce more flexibility in the lower back area as well as the legs.

Reach down and take hold of your ankles (or calves if that is as far as you can reach) and apply gentle pressure to get the fullest possible stretch. Hold at the bottom, then raise slowly back to the starting position.

Try doing this movement on a series of 4 counts: 4 to bend forward, hold for 4, and 4 more beats to come back up.

Repetitions:
5

WARM-DOWNS

2. Seated Hamstring Stretches

This is a seated version of the last exercise and is a little more difficult since you don't have gravity working for you.

The Exercise
Sit on the floor, legs straight out together in front of you. Bend forward, keeping the back straight, and grab hold of your ankles, or as far down the leg as you can.

Gently pull to get the maximum stretch. Keep your toes pulled up and back, rather than pointed, for the greatest stretching effect.

Release, and come back to a sitting position. Use the same 4 counts that you did in the previous exercise.

Repetitions:
5

Date & Reps	Date & Reps

WARM-DOWNS

3. Alternate Seated Hamstring Stretches

This is a variation of the previous exercise, to be done after completing the Seated Hamstring Stretches.

The Exercise

Reach out with your left hand and try to touch your right foot. Hold this position for a couple of beats, then come back to the starting position and try to touch your right hand to your left foot.

Repetitions:
20 with each hand

Date & Reps	Date & Reps

4. Legs-Apart Seated Hamstring Stretches

Now that you have loosened up the hamstrings and lower back, you can begin a more difficult movement that also works the muscles along the side of the torso.

The Exercise

Sit on the floor as for the previous two exercises, only this time spread your legs as wide apart as you can. As you get more limber, you will find you are able to separate your legs more widely. Until then, just get as much stretch as you can, and concentrate on keeping your legs straight, knees locked.

Keeping the back straight, lean forward and touch your hands to the floor as far in front of you as possible.

Now walk your hands along the floor to the left and take hold of your left ankle. Pull gently and as low as you can without bending your back. Hold for a few beats.

Let go of your ankle, walk your hands across to the right, and repeat the same procedure on the other side.

Repetitions:
10 to each side

5. Side Bend Toe Touches

Now that you have loosened up the muscles of the torso, you are ready to stretch them a little farther.

The Exercise

Remain seated on the floor, legs spread as wide apart as possible.

Raise your right hand over your head, turn your torso slightly to the right, then bend over toward the left as far as you can, trying to touch the right hand to the left foot.

Hold this position for a few beats, come back to the starting position, and repeat the movement to the other side.

Make certain that you are bending to the *side* as you do this exercise, not twisting slightly so that you are bending slightly to the front.

Repetitions:
10 to each side

Date & Reps	Date & Reps
————	————
————	————
————	————
————	————
————	————
————	————
————	————
————	————
————	————
————	————
————	————
————	————
————	————
————	————
————	————
————	————
————	————
————	————
————	————
————	————

6. Inner Thigh Stretches

The preceding exercises have primarily worked the back of the legs and the lower back. This movement stretches out the muscles and tendons of the inner thighs.

The Exercise

Sit on the floor and draw your feet toward you and together so that the soles touch.

Hold on to your feet and lower your knees to either side as far as you can. Use your arms to put gentle pressure on your legs and get the fullest possible stretch.

Release the pressure, then reapply it and hold for a count of 5.

Repetitions:
10 pressure/release combinations

Date & Reps	Date & Reps

7. Quadriceps Stretches

This movement is for the quadriceps, the front of the thighs.

Date & Reps	Date & Reps

The Exercise

Kneel on the floor, feet slightly wider apart than your hips. The knees should be as close together as possible. The closer the knees are, the more difficult and effective the exercise.

Put your hands on the floor beside your knees and gently lower your buttocks as far as you can between your feet.

If you can't lower yourself all the way to the floor, continue to hold this position. If you are able to get to the floor, then gradually lean back and try to rest your weight on your elbows.

For those with greater flexibility, continue to lean back bringing your head as close to the floor as possible.

Hold your position for a few moments, or as long as is comfortable. Don't try to go farther than you can in this exercise. Just find your own limit of flexibility. Come back up to your knees, then repeat the stretch two more times, holding it a little longer on each repetition.

Everyday Stretching

Although I only recommend training with weights three days a week with this program, I also think that doing some stretching and flexibility moves every day is a good idea.

On those days during which you are not doing weight training, spend a few minutes doing the pre-workout or post-workout stretching moves. Tension is a part of modern life, and these exercises do a lot to combat tension.

Also, since no equipment is necessary, you can do them anywhere, even in a hotel room. So try to get in the habit of doing some stretching movements every day of your life the way I do. It's really worth the effort.

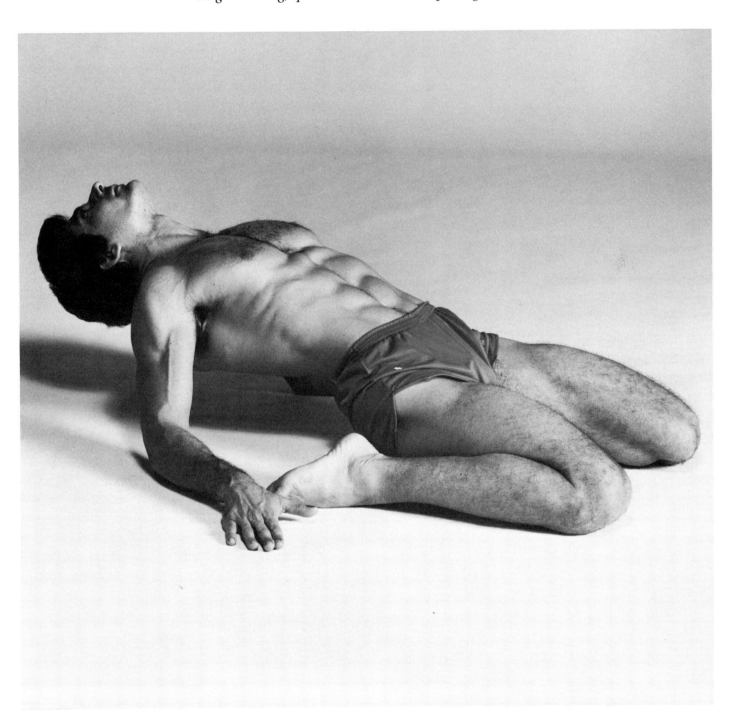

The Exercise Series: How the Program Works

Weight training for shaping and strengthening the body depends on the concept of "progressive resistance." When you lift a weight over and over, your muscles eventually get used to this amount of effort and stop developing. To keep making progress, you have to continue to increase the amount of weight you use in your routines.

The same thing is true of the cardiovascular system. As you increase the speed and intensity with which you go through your workouts, you put added demands on your heart and lungs to supply oxygen to your muscles. This forces them to adapt and become more efficient, which increases your endurance.

However, your progress should be gradual and your routines geared to what your body is really ready for. No use in over-training and breaking down the muscles instead of building them up.

Therefore, I have designed a three-level program, each level more demanding than the one before, designed to allow you to progress as fast as your body is capable of doing.

Series I exercises are designed to firm and condition the body, burn off excess fat, and accustom all your muscles to the demands of weight training.

Series II routines call for an increase in intensity which quickly develops your cardiovascular capacity and gives you a marked increase in endurance.

Series III not only gives you additional exercises, but shows you new ways of putting them together into routines to suit your own needs. In addition it provides the exercises you will need to concentrate on developing specific body parts, as your individual goals may require.

The Most Common Mistake

Success breeds success. Once you begin a program and start to see results, it motivates you to keep on going and try for even greater benefits.

But the opposite can also be true. If you end up with nothing to show for hours of hard work and effort, it can be pretty discouraging. This can make it very difficult to persuade yourself to keep on with your training.

The key is to read the instructions carefully and follow them explicitly. Don't skim over the material. It is essential to do each exercise properly.

At a seminar recently I called a young man up from the audience to do an exercise I had just demonstrated. When he picked up the weights I could see he hadn't the slightest idea how to do the movement. Now, I was there to correct him—but what if he had been trying to learn weight training from one of my books?

It Works!

The weight training system I'm giving you in this book works. But it's up to you to study the program carefully and do exactly what it says. This training system is the end product of thousands of hours of learning, experience, research and experimentation. Stick with it and it will do wonders for your physique, and your whole outlook on life, as well.

And that is all it takes—read the book, master the basics, stick with your training. You'll never regret it.

PART III
SERIES I

In Series I you will be introduced to two exercises per body part (except for calves and abdominals). You will do the two movements one right after another without stopping, then rest briefly and do another two in a row. This is called *Supersetting*.

The following are the Series I exercises:

Stretching:

1. Neck Rolls	5	rolls to each side	**38**
2. Side Bends	10	times to each side	**40**
3. Lunges/Achilles Stretches	5	combinations to one side	**42**
4. Combination Hamstring Stretches	5	stretches to each side	**44**
5. Lunges/Achilles Stretches	5	combinations to opposite side	**46**

Warm-ups:

1. Standing Twists	20	to each side	**48**
2. Bent-Over Twists	20	to each side	**50**
3. Windmills	20	to each side	**52**
4. High Knees	20	with each leg	**54**
5. Jumping Lunges	20	of each position	**56**

Weight Training:

Shoulders:	Clean and Press	8–10 reps	**74**
	Dumbbell Laterals	8–10 reps	**76**
Chest:	Bench Press	8–10 reps	**78**
	Dumbbell Flys	8–10 reps	**80**
Back:	Chin-ups	20 reps	**82**
	Bent-Over Rows with Barbell	8–10 reps	**84**
Arms:	Barbell Curls	8–10 reps	**86**
	Lying Triceps Press	8–10 reps	**88**
Legs:	Squats	8–10 reps	**90**
	Lunges	8–10 reps	**92**
	Standing Calf Raises	15–20 reps	**94**

Abdominals:

1.	Bent-Knee Leg Raises	10 reps	**96**
2.	Bent-Knee Sit-ups (with assistance)	10 reps	**98**
3.	Alternate Knee Kicks	10 reps	**100**
4.	Crunches	10 reps	**102**
5.	Side Knee Raises	10 reps	**104**
6.	Rear Scissors	10 reps	**106**

Warm-downs:

1.	Hamstring Stretches	5 reps	**58**
2.	Seated Hamstring Stretches	5 reps	**60**
3.	Alternate Seated Hamstring Stretches	20 with each hand	**61**
4.	Legs-Apart Seated Hamstring Stretches	10 to each side	**62**
5.	Side Bend Toe Touches	10 to each side	**64**
6.	Inner Thigh Stretches	10 pressure/release combinations	**65**
7.	Quadriceps Stretches	Slow continuous stretch	**66**

How Much?

This entire series of eleven weight training exercises constitutes *one circuit*. Your goal in Series I will be to complete this circuit three times—supersetting two exercises for the same body part, resting, then doing two more and so on until you have gotten through all the movements. (The exceptions to this rule are calf and abdominal training, which I will get to shortly.)

After you have finished one circuit, you will start over and do two additional ones.

How Often?

I recommend that you train at least three days a week, resting at least one day in between exercise days. Thus you might train Monday-Wednesday-Friday; Tuesday-Thursday-Saturday; or any other arrangement that gives you a day of rest after a training day.

How Long?

Once you get used to this program, you will be able to complete your Series I training in less than an hour, including stretching and warm-ups. It will take a little while until you know the exercises so well you can run through them one after another without having to refer to the book. But you might also find yourself tiring after only a few minutes when you first start your training. Don't worry, your conditioning will improve rapidly and it won't be long before you can get through an entire session without exhausting yourself.

How Many Reps?
With too few repetitions of a movement you don't get the fat-burning, conditioning and muscle-shaping benefits from your weight training—If you are doing too many, it means the weights are too light and you are not building enough strength. I recommend training with from 8 to 10 repetitions (except with calves and abs).

If you can't perform at least 8 repetitions of an exercise, the weight you are using is too heavy. If 10 repetitions seem too easy, it is time to increase the weight for that movement.

How Much Weight?
Remember when you are deciding how much weight to put on the bar that you are not just doing one or two lifts, but a whole circuit of exercises. As you get into your second and third circuits, you are going to get tired—and be less able to lift the same weight. Don't worry about it.

This is a program of weight training, not weight-lifting. You get no prizes for lifting more than somebody else. The weights are just a means to an end, and that end is building a physique you can take pride in. Don't let your ego get in the way of your training.

Suggested Weight Ranges
Weight training is, by its nature, self-regulating. As you become accustomed to the program, you will learn what weights are right for you in each exercise, and how quickly you ought to add on more weight.

But, in the beginning, you may not be sure how much weight may be appropriate to use in each of the various exercises. Therefore, I am including with each exercise a suggestion for the minimum and the maximum weight you will probably find comfortable.

Ninety percent of the individuals following this program will probably fall somewhere in this suggested range. However, remember these are only guidelines to help you when you are first getting started. After a few days or weeks, your body itself will tell you whether you ought to be exercising with more or less weight.

This initial stage of training is a good time to really master technique. With lighter weights, get a feel of what the exercise is like, get the movement into a "groove" like a good golf swing, and then try to keep this feeling as you move up to weights that are more challenging.

Strengths and Weaknesses
The human body is made up of a lot of different muscles—more than 600 of them—and in different individuals certain of these muscles are naturally much stronger than others.

This is as true for me as it is for you. When I first picked up a weight I noticed that certain lifts were easier for me than others. I know some bodybuilders who can press a lot of weight but are weak in pulling movements. I know others for whom the opposite is true.

In my case, my problem was with Squats. Because of my structure and physical proportions, I could

Deadlift more than 700 pounds when I was still only 18 years old—without really training for it—but I could never Squat with the enormous weights that some of my training partners used. As a result, I made a point of training twice as hard with my legs as with any other body part and eventually I built my lower body up to Mr. Olympia proportions.

Don't be discouraged if you seem much weaker doing certain of these exercises than you are doing others. I would be surprised if that weren't true. It's just the way the body works. As you keep on with your training, those differences will gradually disappear. Just give it time.

Hints and Shortcuts

It takes time to change the weights on a barbell or dumbbell, and this can slow down your training. But there are a couple of ways to deal with this problem. . . .

(1) In the beginning, while you are still learning the exercises, don't change the weights—pick a comfortable weight for barbell and dumbbells, and stick with that for the entire circuit. This will make some movements relatively too easy, but it will speed up your conditioning and the time it takes to learn the whole series.

(2) When you do begin to change weight for each exercise, try putting what will be the minimum weight you will need inside the collars of the barbell, and then put any additional weight you need for other exercises outside the collars. Most weight sets have plates that fit tightly enough so that they will not slide off the bar as long as you

make some effort not to tip it too far to the side. Obviously, you want to be sure this is true for yours—we don't want you dropping a plate on the floor, or your foot!

This technique works only for the barbell. With dumbbells, you will just have to take the time to change weights each time that is necessary.

Series I Equipment

1 barbell
2 dumbbells—with at least 110 pounds (50 kilos) of interchangeable plates, minimum plate size 2½ pounds.
1 weight bench, preferably with a rack to hold the bar for Bench Presses, ideally having an attachment for Leg Extensions and Leg Curls.
1 chin-up bar
1 full-length mirror (optional)

Abdominal Training

You don't need weights to train abs, and a mere 8–10 reps aren't enough to really condition these muscles. Abdominals are relatively the most neglected muscles in the body, so I am giving you a separate program to work this area of the body.

The benefits of good abdominal training are no secret—a trim, slender waistline, broader looking chest and shoulders, a younger and more attractive appearance.

There is nothing that makes you look so much as if you are in good condition as hard, well-defined abdominals. In a bathing suit, especially, good abs are extremely impressive. The abs are the center of the body, and even back in the time of the Greeks sculptors created their heroic figures will well-developed abdominals.

But, aside from looks, the muscles of the abdomen also function to help support your internal organs, and so you stand to gain in overall health when they are strong and in good condition.

Despite what many people believe, ab work can be very enjoyable. The program I have worked out uses a variety of different movements to help keep things interesting.

When to Train Abs?

Abdominal training should be included in each of your exercise sessions. You have a choice of doing them . . .

(1) before you do your weight-training circuits,
(2) after you have finished your circuits,
(3) in between your circuits.

Abs Every Day

Just as with your stretching exercises, there is no reason to limit your abdominal training to three times a week. I recommend that you do some ab work every single day, and that includes when you are traveling and staying in hotels. Since you don't need any equipment for ab exercises, you can do them anywhere.

Training with a Partner

I remember once I was training with a famous bodybuilder and we were both trying to push each other, and to psych each other out. He finished one exercise and I asked him, "How many reps did you do?" "Ten," he said with a straight face, but I knew better.

I had counted twelve. So I went on and did fifteen, which made us both laugh.

Training with a partner can be stimulating and make the whole thing a lot more fun. One of you may have an off-day, but it is not very likely that this will happen to both of you at the same time.

A training partner can give the feedback it takes to really motivate you, telling you how well you are doing, recognizing your achievement when you do a really good set or succeed for the first time in lifting more weight than you had thought yourself capable of. A little praise at the right time can go a long way.

A partner can push you to greater efforts, and stand by to "spot" you so that you can attempt heavy lifts with confidence. If there is somebody around you can share your training with, by all means get together.

Clean and Press

Purpose: *To increase the strength and thickness of the deltoid (shoulder) muscles, as well as working the back, triceps and, to some degree, the entire upper body.*

Any movement which involves lifting something over your head uses the deltoid muscles. The Clean and Press, as the name implies, is a two-part movement. The first part, "cleaning" the weight, is done by lifting the barbell off the floor and bringing it up to shoulder height. The second, the press, involves lifting the barbell from shoulder height straight up overhead as far as you can.

The Exercise
Place the barbell on the floor in front of you. Stand with your feet wide apart enough for good balance. Bend down and grasp the barbell in a palms-down grip, hands slightly farther apart than shoulder width.

Begin the lift by straightening your legs. When the bar is moving, continue the lift by straightening the back and

Date & Reps	Date & Reps

Michael Morris

pulling upward with the arms.

Lift the bar up to shoulder height, then tuck your elbows in and down so that they are directly under the bar, and it is fully supported, just touching the front of your shoulders and chest.

For the second part of the exercise, merely lift the bar straight up overhead and lock out your arms. Keep the weight balanced; don't let it sway forward or back.

From this position, lower the bar back to shoulder level, then down again to the floor with a reverse of the cleaning technique. This entire series of moves constitutes one repetition.

Don't let the weight rest on the floor. Just lower it, then prepare to lift it again in the next repetition.

Incidentally, cleaning a weight involves a fairly complex technique, so it is best to start out with a light weight until you get the hang of it. And with this or any other exercise that involves lifting while bent over, always use the legs to start the weight off the floor to avoid putting too much stress on the lower back.

Repetitions:
8 to 10
Suggested weight range:
20 to 40 pounds

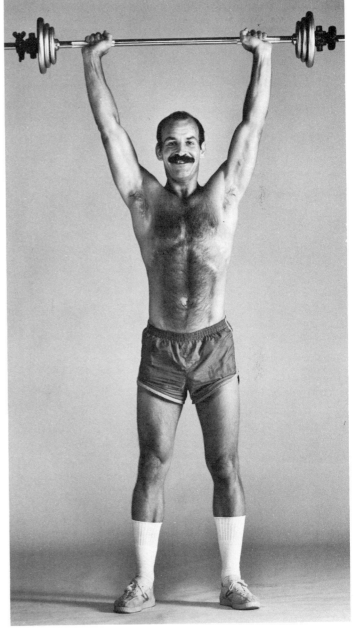

Dumbbell Laterals

Purpose: *To fill out, shape and broaden the shoulders.*

The Exercise
Stand upright, feet a few inches apart, arms at your sides. Hold a dumbbell in each hand, palms turned in toward the body.

Keeping your arms straight, lift the weight out and up to either side until they are about level with the top of your head. From this position, lower them slowly back to your sides.

It is important that you keep the palms turned downward as you do this lift, so that the deltoids do the work rather than the biceps. The correct feeling is almost as if you were pouring water out of a kettle.

Also, make sure you lift the dumbbells on the way up rather than "swing" them. And when you lower them, keep them under control. When you let them drop you are missing half the benefit of the exercise.

Repetitions:
8 to 10
Suggested weight range:
5 to 15 pounds

Date & Reps   **Date & Reps**

CHEST

Bench Press

Purpose: *To strengthen the pectoral muscles; also, to work the deltoids and triceps.*

It is possible to prepare to do Bench Presses by sitting on the bench, the bar across your lap, and then lying back and bringing the weight up to your chest. But a weight you can do this with comfortably is usually too light to really give your chest a workout.

If you are training with a partner, you can have him hand you the weight while you are supine on the bench. But the best way to do this exercise is by using a bench that has supports to hold the bar, as in the illustration.

The Exercise
Lie on the bench and grasp the bar, hands slightly farther apart than shoulder width. Don't lie too far under the bar. It should be just about even with the top of your head.

Date & Reps	Date & Reps

Lift the bar off the rack and hold it straight up, elbows locked. Lower the bar deliberately toward your chest, letting it touch just below the collar bone. Press it back up to the starting position.

The Bench Press seems like a simple strength exercise, but it really involves a great deal of timing and technique. You'll find you improve rapidly after some weeks of practice.

Incidentally, to avoid having to worry about lowering the weight down and not being able to lift it off your chest, it is helpful to have somebody standing by to spot you. This allows you to go for a set of heavy reps when you feel like it without any worries or distractions.

Repetitions:
8 to 10
Suggested weight range:
80 to 120 pounds

Dumbbell Flys

Purpose: *To isolate and train the pectoral muscles.*

The Exercise
Lie on your back on the bench. Take a dumbbell in each hand and hold them straight up overhead, elbows locked. Turn your palms toward one another and bring the dumbbells together.

Lower the dumbbells out to each side in as wide an arc as you can until they are just below the level of the bench, palms facing upward. Feel the stretch in the pectorals.

Date & Reps **Date & Reps**

Squeeze the pectoral muscles together and raise the dumbbells back to the starting position, keeping them in the same wide arc. The feeling is as if you are giving someone a big hug.

The plane in which the dumbbells move should be even with your shoulders. Don't let them drift down toward your waistline.

Repetitions:
8 to 10
Suggested weight range:
8 to 20 pounds

Chin-ups

Purpose: *To work the lats (upper back), as well as the shoulders and biceps to some degree.*

Chin-ups are one of the few movements you do with your own body weight. That means you can't adjust the stress of the exercise downward if you find it too difficult. Individuals differ so much in strength and body weight that some find this exercise much harder than do others. Many can only manage one or two repetitions.

If this is the case with you, I have a suggestion. Do a rep or two and then rest for a few moments. When you have recuperated, do a couple more. You will be surprised how easy it is to do your whole set in just a few minutes this way. However, if you do use this method, try for a total of 20 repetitions instead of the usual 10 to compensate for the relative lack of intensity.

Date & Reps	Date & Reps
———	———
———	———
———	———
———	———
———	———
———	———
———	———
———	———
———	———
———	———
———	———
———	———
———	———
———	———
———	———
———	———

Jon Jon Park: Former Olympic swimmer for England who now lives in South Africa and is a trainer for the South African National Swim Team

Another possibility is to have your training partner hold you at the waist and give you some added lift when you are too tired to do complete reps on your own.

The Exercise
If you don't have a fixed chinning bar available, place an adjustable one in a suitable doorway and be certain that it and the door jamb will hold your weight.

Grasp the bar with your palms turned toward you. With a regular chinning bar you can keep your hands as far apart as you like; in a doorway you will need to keep them fairly close together.

Lower yourself to arm's length below the bar and curl your feet up behind you. From this position, lift yourself upward until your chin is above the bar, then lower yourself again to full extension.

Repetitions:
total of 20

Bent-Over Rows with Barbell

Purpose: *To develop and strengthen the muscles of the upper and lower back.*

The Exercise
With your feet about shoulder-width apart, bend down and grasp the bar in an overhand grip. Come up until your torso is parallel to the floor, let the weight hang below you and be sure to keep your knees slightly bent.

Staying in the same, bent-over position, lift the weight upward until it touches your stomach. Then lower it once again to the starting position. Don't let the weight rest on the floor between repetitions.

Again, the weak link here is the lower back, so keep the knees bent and don't use too much weight until you are ready for it.

Repetitions:
8 to 10
Suggested weight range:
25 to 60 pounds

Barbell Curls

Purpose: *To develop the biceps.*

The Exercise

Grasp the barbell with a palms-up grip, hands about shoulder-width apart. Stand with your feet comfortably apart and let the bar hang down at arm's length in front of you.

Keep your arms turned so that the inside of the elbow faces forward, and keep your elbows stationary throughout the exercise to provide a fixed pivot point.

Lift the bar forward and up in a wide arc until it reaches a position just below the chin. At the top, give a little extra "cramping" motion to insure full contraction of the biceps.

Lower the weight again to the starting position, keeping to a wide arc, and don't let the weight drop. Throughout this movement, keep your concentration on working the biceps rather than letting your shoulder or back muscles take up any of the strain.

Repetitions:
8 to 10
Suggested weight range:
20 to 45 pounds

Lying Triceps Press

Purpose: *To develop the triceps (back of the upper arm).*

The Exercise
Lie on the bench with your head just even with the end. If your bench has a rack on it, remove it or turn around so that your head is at the other end.

Grasp the bar with a palms-forward grip, hands 4 to 6 inches apart, and raise it straight up overhead, elbows locked out.

Date & Reps   **Date & Reps**

Lower the weight slowly down in an arc toward your forehead. Keep your elbows as close together as possible and try not to let the upper arms move.

When you have lowered the weight as far as you can, and can feel the stretch in your triceps, lift it back up to the starting position.

Repetitions:
8 to 10
Suggested weight range:
15 to 30 pounds

LEGS

Squats

Purpose: *To develop and condition the legs, buttocks, lower back and abdominals.*

Since you begin this exercise holding a heavy barbell on your shoulders, it helps to have a Squat Rack, a device that holds the bar in an elevated position allowing you to get underneath and set your shoulders against the bar.

Your legs are much stronger than your arms and shoulders. So the amount of weight you can lift over your head and down onto your shoulders is probably too light to really give your legs a workout.

Some benches come equipped with a Squat Rack as an accessory, and they are also available free-standing.

The Exercise

Either get underneath the bar and lift it off the rack, or clean it, press it and lower it down behind your head onto your shoulders.

Stand with your feet slightly farther apart than shoulder width, back straight, head up, using your hands to

Date & Reps	Date & Reps

keep the bar balanced on your shoulders.

Bend your knees and lower yourself until your thighs are parallel to the floor. Keep your head up, your back straight, and make sure your feet stay flat on the floor. Don't lift your heels or come up on your toes.

From this point, drive your legs toward the floor and push yourself back up to the starting position.

Don't go down below the point where your thighs are parallel to the floor, since this puts too much strain on the knees. Another thing to be careful of is letting yourself drop too quickly and

then "bouncing" at the bottom to maintain momentum. This, too, puts too much strain on the knees, as well as the lower back. Go down and up smoothly and under control, concentrating on balance.

Incidentally, this is another exercise in which it helps to have a partner spot you. Also,

some people are more comfortable if they rest their heels on a one-inch-high piece of wood or some other slight elevation for help in balancing.

Repetitions:
8 to 10
Suggested weight range:
50 to 120 pounds

LEGS

Lunges

Purpose: *To develop the quadriceps (the front of the thigh).*

This exercise is normally done with the barbell held across your shoulders as for Squats. But this movement puts quite a bit of strain on the groin area, and I think it is a good idea to begin by doing it without weights, and wait until you have gotten used to it before trying it with the barbell.

The Exercise
Stand with your feet together, hands on your hips. Step forward with your right foot, bend your right knee and lower yourself toward the floor. Your back should be straight throughout the movement, and you should keep your left leg as straight as you can. Continue down until

Date & Reps	Date & Reps

your left knee almost touches the floor, then push back up to the starting position.

Repeat the movement, this time stepping forward with the left foot, and continue to alternate right and left.

The farther forward you step, the more difficult the exercise. Once you are com- fortable doing a full set of Lunges with a long stride, you can begin using the barbell. Put it across your shoulders just as you would for Squats, but you will find you will need to use much less weight for this movement.

Repetitions:
8 to 10
Suggested weight range:
15 to 35 pounds

Standing Calf Raises

Purpose: *To develop the calf muscles.*

Calves and abdominals are trained somewhat differently from the rest of the body. Because the calves are constantly being forced to sustain your entire weight when you walk or run, they respond to training relatively slowly. It is necessary to "bomb" them, to give them a more than normal dose of reps and sets.

Therefore, I recommend that you do 15 to 20 repetitions of Calf Raises in each set, and do at least three sets at a time. If you want to give them even more of a workout, try doing three sets at the beginning of your workout, and three more later on.

The Exercise
Take a heavy dumbbell in one hand and use your free hand to hold on to something for balance—a chair, for example, a wall or even your bench.

Stand with your toes on a telephone book, or some other elevation, with your heels hanging off the edge. A step of a stairway works fine for this, too.

Gradually lower your heels as far as you can, feeling the stretch in the calf muscles. When you can't go down any farther, raise back up and go as high on your toes as you possibly can. In all cases, you want to get the maximum possible range of motion.

You know you are getting a good calf workout when you feel the "burn" in the

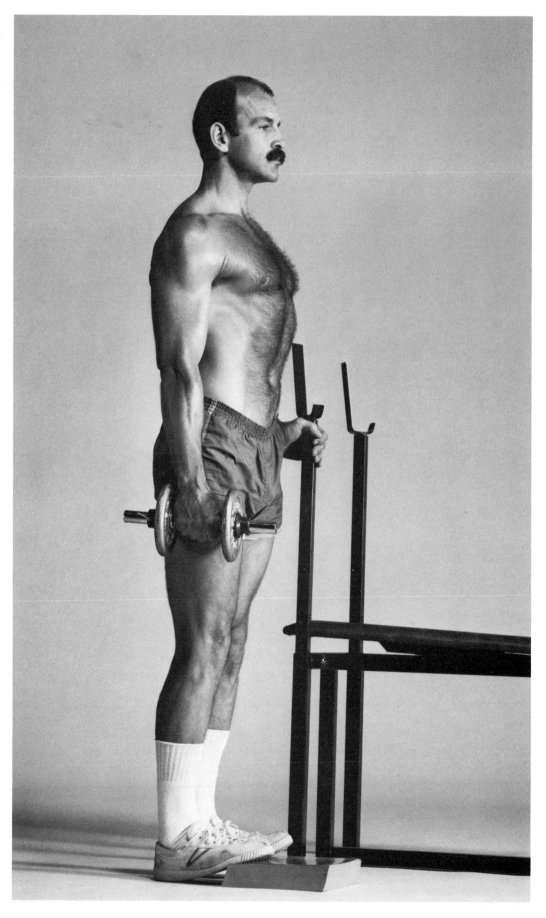

muscle that comes from doing a few extra reps after you are already fatigued.

After you have finished your set, put the weight down and stretch out the calf muscles as far as you can, letting the heels really dip down.

Repetitions:
15 to 20
Suggested weight range:
As much as you can hold securely in one hand

Date & Reps	Date & Reps

ABDOMINALS

Just as with calves, the abs get special treatment. Abdominals are very strong, but they work only in a very limited range of motion. This makes them difficult to train, because it is hard to subject them to the intensity of effort that it takes to get them to respond.

So what I've done is design a program for Series One which involves 60 repetitions of abdominal work: 6 different exercises, 10 repetitions of each, done one right after another without stopping.

Once you've learned the movements and can get through them without stopping, try getting through them in a shorter period of time, picking up the pace and intensity to force the muscles to adapt to the effort.

1. Bent-Knee Leg Raises

Lie on your back, legs straight out, hands under your buttocks, palms flat on the floor for support. Raise your head and shoulders off the floor a few inches, and keep them there throughout the exercise.

Raise your legs, bend your knees, and try to bring them as close to your head as possible. Then straighten your legs again and lower them, but don't let them quite touch the floor.

In all these abdominal exercises, exhale and suck in your stomach whenever you contract your abs. This lines up the muscles and lets you use them to maximum effect.

ABDOMINALS

2. Bent-Knee Sit-ups (with assistance)

Traditional, straight-leg Sit-ups put too much stress on the lower back, so I recommend you do your Sit-ups with bent knees instead.

Lie on your back, knees bent, feet flat on the floor. Fold your hands behind your neck or head.

Begin by lifting up your head and shoulders and coming forward as far as you can. At the same time, throw your arms forward to help in the effort, and touch your chin to your knees.

Hold for a moment, then lower yourself back to the floor and put your hands back behind your head.

ABDOMINALS

3. Alternate Knee Kicks

Lie on your back, resting on your elbows, legs out straight in front of you, lifted a few inches off the floor.

Bring your right knee as far toward your head as you can, leaving your left leg out straight just above the floor.

Pull your left knee up toward your head, and simultaneously extend your right leg out and back to the starting position.

Continue to work your legs alternately, bringing one knee back as you push the other leg forward.

Bringing the right knee up, and then the left, constitutes one full repetition.

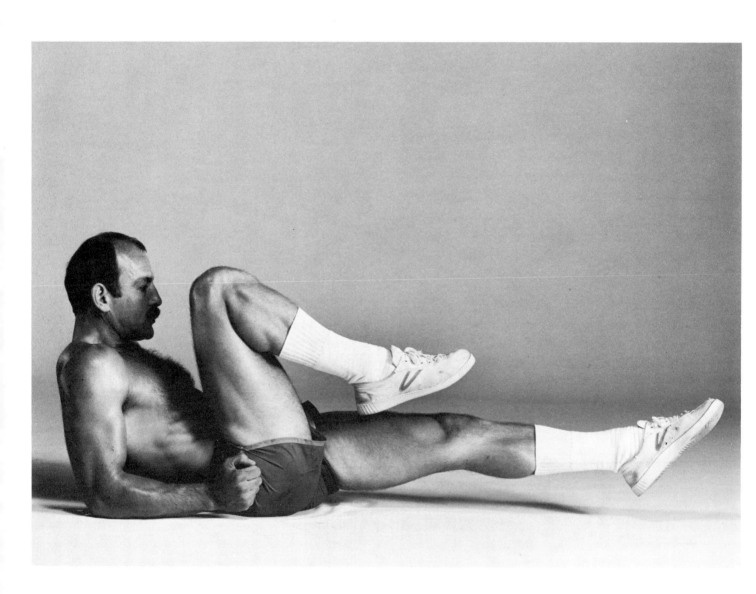

ABDOMINALS

4. Crunches

Lie on your back on the floor. Put your hands behind your head, then bring both knees up together as far as you can and hold this position.

Lift your head and torso and try to come as close to your stationary knees as possible. Hold this position for a moment, then lower your torso back to the floor. Don't let your head rest when you are in the lower position.

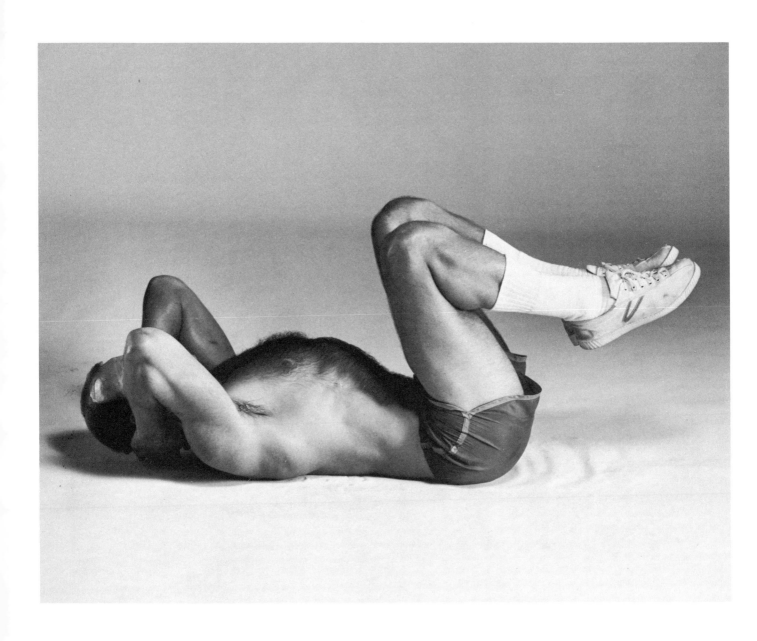

ABDOMINALS

5. Side Knee Raises

This is an exercise for your waist.

Lie on your right side, supporting yourself on your elbow. Hold your left leg out straight and bend your right leg in underneath it.

Draw up your left leg, bending your knee, and try to touch the knee to your left shoulder. Hold for a moment, then return it to the starting position.

After ten repetitions of this movement, turn over on your left side and repeat the exercise with your right leg.

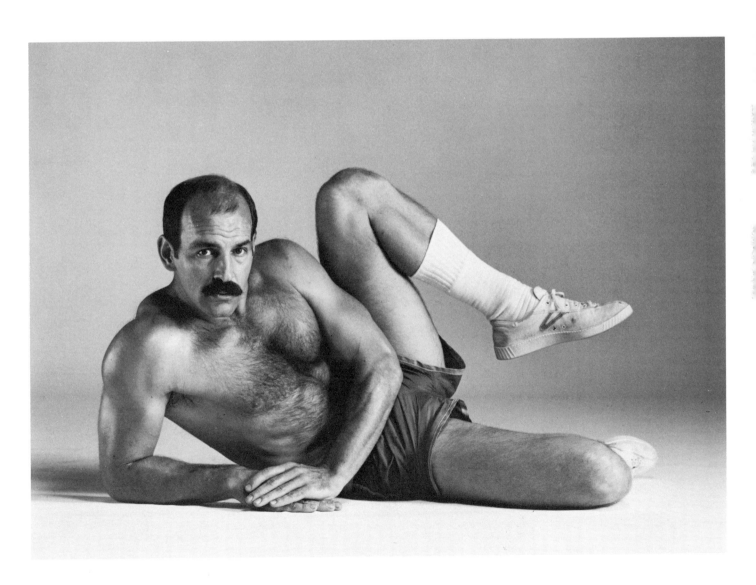

6. Rear Scissors

Date & Reps	Date & Reps

This is a lower back rather than an abdominal exercise, but it is very important for its effect on the waistline.

Lie on your stomach and put your hands under your hip bones for support. Raise your legs up behind you as far as comfortable, and try to keep them straight.

Using a circular motion, cross your right leg over and your left leg under, creating a scissors movement. Then reverse the movement, crossing the left over the right.

During this exercise, don't let your thighs touch the floor. Once over with each leg constitutes one full repetition.

PART IV
SERIES II

When to Move On

It is time to go from Series I to Series II when:

(1) You have memorized all the exercises and can go through your workout without looking any of them up.

(2) You notice a gain in strength of at least 25% in all the movements measured by the weight you are able to lift.

(3) You are able to get through your entire workout in a reasonable amount of time (significantly less than when you began) without becoming badly out of breath.

The Intensity Factor

Intensity is the key to progressive resistance training. To keep the body responding, you need to keep "upping the ante." You have to make the muscles work harder. There are several ways of doing this.

(1) Adding more weight. . . . Obviously, if what you are after is maximum gain in strength, this is how you would increase the intensity of your training.

(2) Adding more exercises. . . . This makes your body do the same work for longer periods, and increases endurance and cardiovascular conditioning.

Unfortunately, the first way doesn't do a lot for conditioning, the second not too much for strength, and both tend to take up longer and longer periods of time. There is, however, a third way. . . .

(3) Do more work in less time.

The Continuous Circuit

Series II is based on the third method referred to above. The first thing we are going to do is get rid of the rest periods between supersets (two exercises done in a row without resting in between). From now on, you will do all the exercises of the weight-training circuit one after another without stopping until the *entire circuit is complete.*

This continuous training is a great step upward in intensity. Because it is so much more demanding, it will do a lot more for improving your strength and conditioning. But you will find that all sorts of adjustments are necessary when you switch from supersets to continuous training. When you go from one exercise to another without stopping, it places much greater demands on the heart and circulatory system than when you stop to rest frequently. These demands result eventually in a higher level of cardiovascular conditioning. But when you first start this kind of training you will tire sooner, and therefore be able to lift less weight. That's normal. Pretty soon you will get used to the new routine and be lifting even more than you did before. Be patient.

The advantage of this method for most people is that you are able to do more in less time, and time is the element that few of us have enough of. Neither you nor I really have time in a busy day for three or four hours of hard training, so a program that stresses intensity rather than duration is a blessing.

Getting into Series II

Your transition from Series I to Series II can be gradual. Begin by doing as many exercises in a row as you possibly can. If you can get through a whole circuit, fine. If you can't quite, then do as much as you are able—and then finish off the rest of your training session doing your familiar supersets.

Keep this up until you are able to go through three continuous circuits of the weight-training exercises, stopping to rest only briefly in between. Once you can do this, begin to increase the weights you use in your exercises.

This gives you a two-fold benefit: increase in conditioning as well as increase in strength. And all this with no more investment in time than you have already learned to set aside for Series I.

Stretching:

1. Neck Rolls	5	rolls to each side	**38**
2. Side Bends	10	times to each side	**40**
3. Lunges/Achilles Stretches	5	combinations to one side	**42**
4. Combination Hamstring Stretches	5	stretches to each side	**44**
5. Lunges/Achilles Stretches	5	combinations to opposite side	**46**

Warm-ups:

1. Standing Twists	20	to each side	**48**
2. Bent-Over Twists	20	to each side	**50**
3. Windmills	20	to each side	**52**
4. High Knees	20	with each leg	**54**
5. Jumping Lunges	20	of each position	**56**

Weight Training:

Shoulders:	Clean and Press	8–10 reps	**74**
	Dumbbell Laterals	8–10 reps	**76**
Chest:	Bench Press	8–10 reps	**78**
	Dumbbell Flys	8–10 reps	**80**
Back:	Chin-ups	20 reps	**82**
	Bent-Over Rows with Barbell	8–10 reps	**84**
Arms:	Barbell Curls	8–10 reps	**86**
	Lying Triceps Press	8–10 reps	**88**
Legs:	Squats	8–10 reps	**90**
	Lunges	8–10 reps	**92**
	Standing Calf Raises	15–20 reps	**94**

Abdominals:

1. *Straight Leg Raises/	10 reps	
Bent-Knee Leg Raises	10 reps	**112**
2. *Bent-Knee Sit-ups (without assistance)/	10 reps	
Bent-Knee Sit-ups (with assistance)	10 reps	**114**
3. *Alternate Leg Flutters/	10 reps	
Alternate Knee Kicks	10 reps	**116**
4. *Twisting Crunches/	10 reps	
Crunches	10 reps	**118**
5. *Side Leg Raises/	10 reps	
Side Knee Raises	10 reps	**120**
6. *Rear Flutters/	10 reps	
Rear Scissors	10 reps	**122**

* indicates new exercise

110

Warm-downs:

ABDOMINALS

The abdominal program for Series II is an extension of the one you have already learned in Series I. But these new exercises are compound movements. *They combine the exercise you have already mastered with a variation of that exercise, done in one continuous series of repetitions.*

Since you are supersetting two exercises, you will be doing 20 repetitions instead of 10, and this is obviously more difficult. However, although it does call for a greater degree of intensity, the second part of each exercise is designed to be easier than the first, to compensate for the fatigue you will be feeling.

Don't worry if you can't get through the entire program at first—6 exercises, 20 reps each, is obviously a lot of work. The abs adapt quickly, and you will soon be able to breeze through the program without difficulty.

1. Straight Leg Raises/ Bent-Knee Leg Raises

Lie flat on your back, your hands under your buttocks, palms down, for support. Lock your legs out straight, and lift them and your head a few inches off the floor.

Keeping your legs straight, raise them as high off the floor as you can, then lower than down again, but don't let them touch the floor.

Do 10 repetitions of this exercise, then follow with 10 Bent-Knee Leg Raises. (See page 96.)

David Kingsdale: A Southern California high-school student

2. Bent-Knee Sit-ups (without and with assistance)

Lie on your back, knees drawn up, feet flat on the floor. Hold your hands behind your neck.

Sit up, trying to touch your chin to your knees, and leave your hands in position behind your neck. Hold for a moment, then lower yourself back to the floor, but don't let your head touch.

After 10 repetitions, follow with 10 assisted Sit-ups, that is, letting your hands come forward to give you added leverage. (See page 98.)

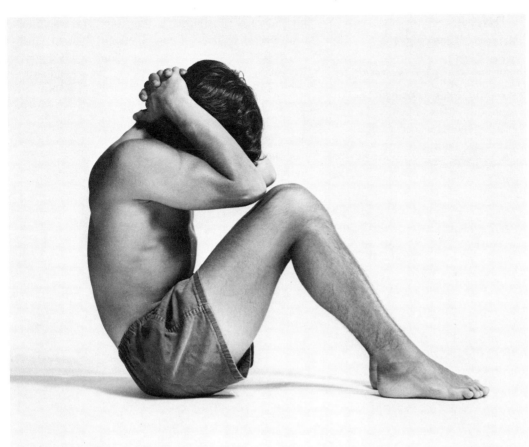

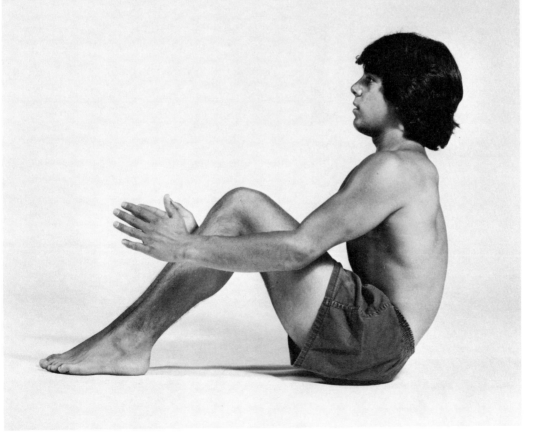

3. Alternate Leg Flutters/Alternate Knee Kicks

Lie on your back, your hands under your buttocks palms down for support. Keep your legs straight, and raise your feet and head slightly off the floor.

Keeping your legs straight, raise the left one as high as you can. The right leg should remain where it is.

From this position, simultaneously raise the right leg and lower the left leg back to the starting position. Repeat this "flutter" movement 10 times with each leg.

After your 10 reps, come up onto your elbows and do 10 repetitions of Alternate Knee Kicks. (See page 100.)

4. Twisting Crunches/ Crunches

Lie on your back, hands behind your neck, and raise your feet slightly off the floor.

Keeping your right leg straight, bend your left knee and pull it as far up toward your head as you can. At the same time, raise and twist your upper body and try to touch your right elbow to your left knee.

Come back down, straighten your left leg, not letting it touch the floor, and bring your right knee up, again lifting and twisting the upper body and trying to touch the knee with your left elbow.

Do 10 repetitions with each leg, then draw both knees up, hold them stationary, and do 10 repetitions of Crunches. (See page 102.)

5. Side Leg Raises/Side Knee Raises

Lie on your left side, right leg out straight, left leg bent underneath it for balance. Lift your right leg straight up from the hip, until foot is pointing at ceiling if possible, keeping the knee as straight as you can.

When you've raised it as high as you can, lower it slowly, but don't let it touch.

Do 10 repetitions of this movement, then bend the knee and do 10 Side Knee Raises. (See page 104.)

Turn over onto your right side, and repeat the same combination of movements.

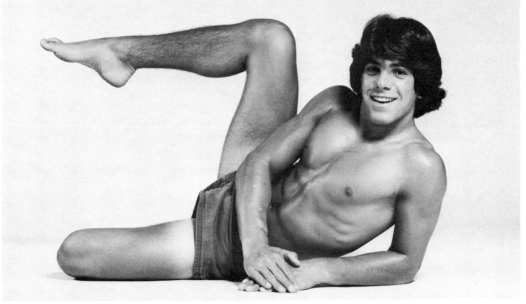

6. Rear Flutters/ Rear Scissors

Lie on your stomach, your head off the floor, and put your hands under your pelvis for support. Keep your legs out straight behind you, and lift them slightly off the floor.

Raise one leg as high as you can. From this position, lower it again to the starting position, simultaneously lifting the other one. This flutter motion is a lot like one you would use in swimming, but the legs remain straight.

After 10 Flutters with each leg, follow with 10 reps of Rear Scissors. (See page 106.)

Date & Reps   Date & Reps

123

PART V
SERIES III
Taking the Next Step

The whole point of progressive-resistance training is that you have to keep challenging your body as it becomes used to any level of effort. You have to keep giving it more to do. It's just as Alice found out in her journey in Wonderland—sometimes you have to run faster and faster just to stay in the same place.

In weight training, you can't just keep doing the same thing. Somewhere along the line, you have to train with more intensity. Either you need to lift more weight, to go through your routine at a faster pace, to add more exercises to your program—or all of the above.

So you can't stay at Series II indefinitely. Sooner or later, you will want to take the next step. I think you ought to consider taking that step:

(1) When you have developed enough conditioning that three Series II continuous circuits are no longer any real problem for you to get through.
(2) And when you've noticed a significant (25% to 50%) gain in strength.

When these two changes have come about, you could continue just to add more weight for each exercise, but you'll make even faster progress if you "shock" the body by making new demands on it, giving it something unfamiliar to do and forcing it to make further adaptations. That's when it's time for Series III.

Introducing Series III

Series III involves a very sophisticated program. Instead of eleven weight-training movements, you will be doing twenty-two, twice as many. And, instead of three complete circuits, you will eventually work up to four.

There are more abdominal exercises to work with, too, since a good, hard set of abdominals is the pride and glory of any man who really considers himself to be in shape.

The exercises in the following list include those you have already mastered in Series I and Series II, which will continue to play an important role in your training, as well as the new exercises you will be learning in Series III:

Stretching:

1. Neck Rolls	5	rolls to each side	38
2. Side Bends	10	times to each side	40
3. Lunges/Achilles Stretches	5	combinations to one side	42
4. Combination Hamstring Stretches	5	stretches to each side	44
5. Lunges/Achilles Stretches	5	combinations to opposite side	46

Warm-ups:

1. Standing Twists	20	to each side	48
2. Bent-Over Twists	20	to each side	50
3. Windmills	20	to each side	52
4. High Knees	20	with each leg	54
5. Jumping Lunges	20	of each position	56

Weight Training:

Shoulders:	Clean & Press	8–10 reps	**74**
	Dumbbell Laterals	8–10 reps	**76**
	*Upright Rows	8–10 reps	**130**
	*Bent-Over Lateral Raises	8–10 reps	**132**
Chest:	Bench Press	8–10 reps	**78**
	Dumbbell Flys	8–10 reps	**80**
	*Dumbbell Press	8–10 reps	**134**
	*Pullovers	8–10 reps	**136**
Back:	Chin-ups	20 reps	**82**
	Bent-Over Rows with Barbell	8–10 reps	**84**
	*One-Arm Rows	8–10 reps	**138**
	*Deadlifts	8–10 reps	**140**
Arms:	Barbell Curls	8–10 reps	**86**
	Lying Triceps Press	8–10 reps	**88**
	*Dumbbell Curls	8–10 reps	**142**
	*Wrist Curls	8–10 reps	**144**
Legs:	Squats	8–10 reps	**90**
	Lunges	8–10 reps	**92**
	Standing Calf Raises	15–20 reps	**94**
	*Leg Extensions	8–10 reps	**146**
	*Leg Curls	8–10 reps	**148**
	*One-Legged Calf Raises	15–20 reps	**150**

* indicates new exercise

Abdominals:

1. Straight Leg Raises/	10 reps	
Bent-Knee Leg Raises	10 reps	**112**
2. Bent-Knee Sit-ups (without assistance)	10 reps	
Bent-Knee Sit-ups (with assistance)	10 reps	**114**
3. Alternate Leg Flutters/	10 reps	
Alternate Knee Kicks	10 reps	**116**
4. Twisting Crunches/	10 reps	
Crunches	10 reps	**118**
5. Side Leg Raises/	10 reps	
Side Knee Raises	10 reps	**120**
6. Rear Flutters/	10 reps	
Rear Scissors	10 reps	**122**

Supplementary Abdominal Exercises which can be used in addition to or instead of the preceding exercises:

*Cramping Leg Raises	10–20 reps	**152**
*Alternate Leg Kicks	10–20 reps	**154**
*Scissors Leg Raises	10–20 reps	**156**
*Circular Leg Raises	10–20 reps	**158**
*Super Crunches	10–20 reps	**160**

Warm-downs:

1. Hamstring Stretches	5 reps	**58**
2. Seated Hamstring Stretches	5 reps	**60**
3. Alternate Seated Hamstring Stretches	20 with each hand	**61**
4. Legs-Apart Seated Hamstring Stretches	10 to each side	**62**
5. Side Bend Toe Touches	10 to each side	**64**
6. Inner Thigh Stretches	10 pressure/release combinations	**65**
7. Quadriceps Stretches	slow continuous stretch	**66**

* indicates new exercise

Making the Transition

The change from Series II to Series III can, and probably should, be gradual. After all, you have to learn the new exercises, and you need to get used to a much higher level of effort.

Therefore, I would go about making the transition in this manner:

(1) Do a continuous circuit of the familiar exercises, rest for a few moments, then do the new circuit by supersetting the movements the way you did in Series I. Repeat this procedure for a total of four circuits.

(2) When you can do all of the new exercises without looking them up, try following your continuous circuit of familiar exercises with a continuous circuit of the new ones. Go through them as far as your endurance will allow. If you can't quite get through four circuits this way, then finish off by supersetting as many of the new exercises that are remaining as you can.

(3) You have mastered Series III when you can do four complete circuits with a minimum of rest in between. At this point you can start working on adding weight to the movements and cutting back on the length of time it takes you to get through the program.

How Much Weight?

Obviously, if you are going to be doing a lot more work, you are going to get more tired—and this usually means using less weight in some of the exercises. Don't let this bother you. It doesn't represent any kind of step backward in your progress. But some people get hung up on the idea of how much they can lift, and they begin to feel that it does.

So let me remind you that weight training is not the same as weightlifting. Once you've gotten used to the intensity of effort in Series III, you will see yourself making even faster gains in strength. Be patient, and use the appropriate amount of weight on each of the exercises so that you can get through four circuits without any kind of cheating.

The Next Step

Many people begin by training at home and then become so interested in weight training that they join a gym or a health club. Certainly, you can do a lot of things in a well-equipped gym that would be difficult at home. The exercises in this book are all among the ones that I use when training in a gym, so what you learn here will never be wasted, no matter how far you decide to go.

But a word of caution: if you do decide to join a gym, don't get rid of your home training equipment. Remember, there may be times when getting to the gym may be difficult or inconvenient. At those times, being able to train at home instead might mean the difference between being able to train that day or missing your workout entirely.

Adapting Series III Exercises for Specialized Training

Weight training is marvelous in the way it can be used for specialized, individual purposes, as well as for a general program of physical development and conditioning. There is no other kind of fitness program that I know of that has the same capabilities.

Take for instance a case where you have decided to train to improve your tennis game. Tennis involves a lot of quick moves, running short distances, stopping, turning and changing direction. Stopping involves using the quadriceps muscles, so you might want to do a lot of Leg Extensions. Quick changes of direction mean good calf muscles, and those can be developed by adding more Calf Raises to your routines.

But upper body development is important, too. Look at Jimmy Connors or Rod Laver and you'll see that the arm they use to wield the racquet is much bigger than the other. That means bigger muscles and more strength on that side. It took them years of playing to develop that arm, but you can give yourself a head start simply by working the deltoid, upper arm, forearm and wrist with weights.

There is a thing called "specificity of training." This means that the only way to really train for something is to practice that particular thing. Training with weights won't make you a great tennis player, but it will give you the basic strength and conditioning, and then it is up to you to train for the specific sport or activity you're interested in.

Individualized Training

All it takes to individualize your training is just to do the particular exercises you are interested in, or to plan your weight training circuits so that they contain more exercises for certain body parts than for others. It's as simple as that.

I never recommend, even when you are working to develop a specific muscle or muscle group, that you ignore the rest of the body. All I am talking about is altering the *ratio* of certain exercises to your entire workout. By all means, specialize if you need to, but don't let the rest of the body go downhill. Sooner or later, you will suffer for this, since the body is really one interconnected organism.

Rehabilitation

Sometimes the need arises for specialized training because of an injury to the body or the inability to perform certain kinds of movements. For example, I have a friend who has a problem with his shoulder joint. He can lift his arm straight up overhead, but not out to the side and up. Therefore, I advised him to do Shoulder Presses, but to avoid trying to do Lateral Raises. Because of the adaptability of weight training, he is able to work around his problem and still get a good workout.

Certainly, modern physical therapy uses weight training extensively in strengthening and restoring a full range of motion to injured areas of the body. Anyone with a serious injury should, of course, put himself under the care of a doctor. However, a rule of thumb for dealing with less serious problems such as pulled or strained muscles is this: *if it hurts, don't do it*. However, if you can go through a movement with no weight or with a light weight and experience no pain, you are probably not doing yourself any harm and are on the right track.

In general, if you have any kind of physical problem that gets in your way when you are trying to exercise, try to work around it. Try different movements for that body part, or, in more severe cases, avoid training that part of the body entirely. But don't let minor problems keep you from training altogether. People with physical difficulties are even more in need of training than anyone else.

Training for Looks

How you look, as I've said, is a very important aspect of your life. When you begin to train with weights, you frequently get some surprises. While the entire body responds to progressive resistance training, some parts adapt more quickly and completely than others. For example, you might find that you have a genetic predisposition for development of the pectoral muscles, while the biceps and triceps in the arm are slower to develop. Therefore, it would make sense for you to add a lot more upper arm work to your training to balance out your proportions.

Some people have naturally well-developed legs, but find producing a proportional development in the upper body is more difficult. This kind of problem is one that weight training is well suited to dealing with. After you have mastered Series III and seen physical changes begin to happen, stop for a moment, take a look in the mirror or study your physique photos, and analyze what you see. Pick out those body parts that you think might need some extra training, and simply do a disproportionate amount of training for that area, without neglecting the rest of the body.

Once you learn how to do this, you have a more complete control over how you look than most people think possible. And, as time goes on, that control comes to be more complete and more sure. You can, given the limitations of your physical structure, pretty much make yourself into whatever you want, make yourself look any way you please. Weight training on this level becomes mind over matter, the idea made flesh.

Let's Get Started

All this is in the future. For now, study, learn and practice the following exercises. And when you begin to see accelerated changes in your body, just remember who "told you so!"

Upright Rows

Purpose: *To develop the trapezius muscles, the upper back and biceps.*

The Exercise

Stand with your feet comfortably apart, bend down and pick up the barbell, hands about six inches apart in an overhand (palms down) grip. Stand up and let the bar hang down at arm's length in front of you.

Begin the exercise by lifting the bar straight upward to a point just below your chin. Your elbows lift out and up as the bar comes up. Try to keep the bar as close to your body as you can at all times. Also, keep the back as straight as you can to prevent the lower back muscles from helping with the lift.

Hold for a moment at the top, then lower the weight once more to the starting position, being careful to keep it under control at all times.

Repetitions:
8 to 10

Daniel Bromstead

Date & Reps	Date & Reps

Bent-Over Lateral Raises

Purpose: *To develop the rear deltoids.*

The deltoids are large, full muscles, and it takes a number of movements to fully develop them. The Shoulder Press trains the front deltoids, the Lateral Raise the sides, and this movement hits the rear deltoids.

You can do this movement standing, but I recommend you try it sitting on a bench. This helps you maintain balance and allows you to concentrate more energy on the exercise.

The Exercise

Sit on the end of your bench, take a dumbbell in each hand, and bend over, letting the dumbbells come nearly together below your knees.

Keeping your arms straight, lift the weights out and up to each side in as wide an arc as possible to a position just above your head. Be sure to stay bent over during the entire movement. Don't aid the lift by straightening up.

Date & Reps	Date & Reps

From the top position, lower the weights again in a wide arc, keeping your arms straight. Resist the downward movement with your deltoids and keep the weights under control. At the bottom, come to a complete stop to ensure that you won't swing the weights up with a "running start."

Repetitions:
8 to 10

Dumbbell Press

Purpose: *To develop the pectoral muscles and, to a degree, the deltoids and triceps.*

When you do virtually the same movement with dumbbells instead of a barbell, it can radically change the effect of the exercise on the body. Both hands work in concert toward the same objective with a barbell. But when you use dumbbells, each hand has to work independently, adding to the problems of balance. Also, using dumbbells allows you to "pronate" or rotate the hand and wrist, which works the muscles at new angles.

The Exercise

Lie on your back on the bench, holding a dumbbell in each hand. Bring the weights to a point just above your shoulders, palms facing forward, elbows pointing out.

Lift the weights simultaneously straight upward until your arms are locked out. Then lower them again to the starting position, feeling the stretch in the pectoral muscles as your elbows drop below the level of the bench.

Repetitions:
8 to 10

Date & Reps   **Date & Reps**

135

Pullovers

Purpose: *To expand the rib cage, give density and depth to the chest.*

The Exercise

Take hold of one dumbbell with both hands, flattening your palms against the inside of one of the plates. Lie on your back *across* a bench. Your shoulders should be on the bench, head hanging off one side, and pelvis as low to the ground as possible on the other. Raise the dumbbell directly up overhead. Since you are pressing against the underside of the top plate, the shaft of the dumbbell will be pointing straight down toward you.

Gradually lower the weight in a wide arc toward the floor behind your head. Your arms should remain straight, transmitting the pull directly toward your pectoral muscles and rib cage. Keep your bottom as close to the floor as you can. Raising up takes some of the benefit away from the movement.

When you've lowered the dumbbell as far as you can, raise it up again, pulling with the chest muscles, and keeping the weight moving in a wide arc until it is back to a position straight up overhead.

Repetitions:
8 to 10

Date & Reps	Date & Reps

BACK

One-Arm Rows

Purpose: *To develop the muscles of the upper back, particularly the lats.*

The Exercise

Take a dumbbell in your right hand. Stand with the left foot forward, the right foot back. Bend your knees slightly, and lean down until your torso is about parallel to the floor. Let the weight hang straight down at arm's length.

Put your free hand on a chair or something to give you support and balance. If you find it more comfortable, you can also lean your hand or forearm against your forward knee.

Lift the weight directly up toward your shoulder. Your torso will twist slightly as you lift. Try to feel the pull in your lats throughout this movement.

At the top, lower the weight once more, resisting the pull of the weight and keeping it under control.

After you have done your reps with one arm, switch over and repeat the movement with the other.

Repetitions:
8–10 to each side

Date & Reps   Date & Reps

BACK

Deadlifts

Purpose: *To develop all the muscles of the back, as well as the shoulders, torso, arms and legs.*

This is perhaps the single most beneficial exercise you can do for developing the overall strength of the body. It is your strongest exercise —you can move more weight in a Deadlift than you can with any other kind of lift.

The weak link, still, is the back. This is especially true in this exercise, since you can work with so much weight. Therefore, it is especially important to pay close attention to technique as you begin to lift heavier weights.

The Exercise
Stand with your feet about shoulder-width apart. Squat down, with a full bend of the knees, and grasp the bar, hands slightly wider apart than your feet. Hold the bar with an overhand grip with one hand, underhand with the other. This will help you to balance the bar and hold firmly as you begin working with more weight.

Your legs should be bent, your back inclined forward, almost straight. The initial

move to lift the weight is made with the legs, not the back. With your arms fully extended, push up with the legs and don't begin to bring the back to a vertical position until the weight is well on its way.

Straighten the legs and stand completely upright. At this point, shrug your shoulders back, as if coming to a position of full attention, chin up, back arched.

As you lower the weight again, be sure to use the power of your legs as much as possible. Squat down, bending the knees, look forward and keep your back as flat as possible as you go forward.

At the bottom, just touch the weight to the floor. Don't let it rest and take the strain off your muscles. After it touches, push up with the legs and do another repetition.

Repetitions:
8 to 10

Date & Reps   **Date & Reps**

ARMS

Dumbbell Curls

Purpose: *To develop the biceps.*

This is another exercise in which substituting dumbbells for a barbell makes a lot of difference. Many people prefer dumbbell curls to barbell curls because they feel that there is less strain on the elbows when they are free to move. I personally like both movements.

The Exercise
Sit on the end of the bench, a dumbbell in each hand. Sit upright, shoulders back and back straight, and hold the dumbbells at arm's length down by your sides. Turn your arms so that the inside of your elbows and your palms face forward.

Bending the elbows but keeping them in place, lift the dumbbells forward and up as close to your shoulders as possible. Don't sway, or let any other muscles besides the biceps help with the lift.

Hold for a moment, then lower them again, resisting the weight and keeping the dumbbells under control. Follow the same arc downward as you did going up, and continue to keep the elbows from moving.

At the bottom, let the weights go to arm's length to fully stretch the biceps.

Repetitions:
8 to 10

Date & Reps	Date & Reps

ARMS

Wrist Curls

Purpose: *To develop the forearms.*

The wrists and forearms get some training when you do other movements, but Wrist Curls are designed to work these areas specifically. The forearms, like the calves, tend to respond very slowly to training. So if you would like to make extra progress in this area, go ahead and include extra set and reps of Wrist Curls in your routine.

The Exercise
Grip the barbell palms up, hands only a few inches apart. Sit straddling the bench, bend forward, and put the back of your forearms down on the bench's surface, with your wrists and hands hanging off the end. Your elbows will fit comfortably and firmly between your thighs, just forward of your knees.

Keeping your forearms firmly on the bench, lower your hands and the bar as far toward the floor as you can. When your wrists are bent as far back as they will go, open your fingers and let the bar roll out of your palm a few inches. Do this carefully so that you keep control of the weight.

At this point, close your fingers and curl the weight back into your palms, then lift your hands as high as they will go, hinging at the wrists. Lower the bar again to complete one repetition.

Repetitions:
8 to 10

Leg Extensions

Purpose: *To develop the quadriceps (the front of the thigh).*

You will need an appropriately equipped bench, like the one in the illustration, to do this exercise and the one following.

The Exercise

Sit flat on the bench and hook your feet under the lower padded bar of the Leg Extension machine. Take hold of the bench with your hands to hold yourself firmly in place.

   Straighten your legs slowly against the resistance of the machine, taking care you don't rise up off the bench. When your legs are locked out straight in front of you, slowly lower the weight down to the starting position.

   Always try for the fullest range of motion you can—all the way up, all the way down—and don't swing the weight to gain momentum, or come up off the bench to improve your mechanical advantage.

Repetitions:
8 to 10

LEGS

Leg Curls

Purpose: *To develop the leg biceps.*

The Exercise

Lie face down on the bench and hook the back of your ankles below the upper padded bar of the machine.

Holding yourself flat on the bench, curl your legs up and bring your feet as close to your buttocks as possible. If you can't get the weight all the way up, try taking off a few plates.

Hold at the top for a moment, then slowly lower the weight back to the starting position, trying for the fullest range of motion possible.

Be sure to lower the weight slowly, resisting its pull all the way. On the way up and going back down, make the muscle do all the work.

Repetitions:
8 to 10

One-Legged Calf Raises

Purpose: *To develop the calves.*

Without using the kinds of machines you find at gyms, it's difficult to put enough stress on the calves to really get them to respond. But when you do your Calf Raises one leg at a time, you double the amount of weight the muscles have to deal with and accelerate their development.

The Exercise

As you would for regular Calf Raises, stand with the balls of the feet resting on a stair, block or telephone book, a dumbbell in one hand, holding on to something for balance.

Take one foot off and hook it behind the ankle of the other leg. Lower the heel of this supporting leg as far toward the floor as possible, then come up on your toes as far as you can.

After you get a good "burn" in this leg, switch legs and repeat the exercises with the other.

Remember to get a full stretch at the bottom, and come all the way onto the toes at the top.

Repetitions:
15–20 to each side

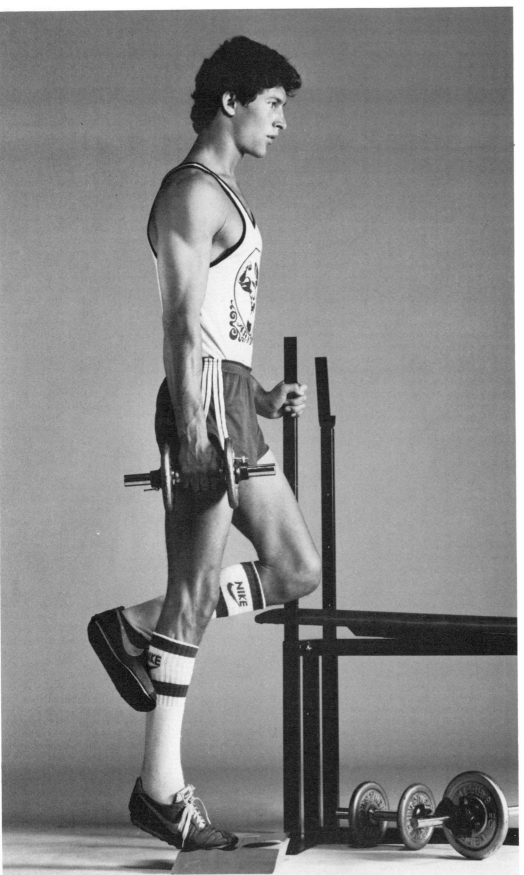

ABDOMINALS

Variety is the spice of life—and of abdominal training. The more variations you can put into your ab training, the more fun you will have and the better your results will be.

These Series III exercises are intended to augment the program you have already learned, not to replace it. You can alternate this set of abdominal exer-cises with the other ones circuit by circuit, or you can double up and try to get through all of them whenever you feel particu-larly motivated.

Many of these exercises differ only slightly from the earlier ones, but those small differences can often be crucial. The more you can surprise your muscles by making unusual and unex-pected demands on them, the more you are going to force them to continue to adapt and respond to train-ing.

Cramping Leg Raises

Sit on the floor, supporting yourself with your hands. Lean back, bend your knees and bring them up as close to your face as possible.

Straighten your legs, keep-ing them as close to the floor as you can without letting them touch the floor. Lean back on your hands as far as you have to to keep your bal-ance.

Bend your knees once more, and pull them up toward your face, and let your body come forward in a "cramping" motion.

Repetitions:
10 to 20

Alternate Leg Kicks

Sit on the floor, your legs out straight in front of you. Straighten your arms out behind you and to the side and lean back for support.

Bend your left leg back, putting your foot flat on the floor. Push up with that leg and raise your buttocks so you are supported only by your arms and the one foot. Keep your right leg out straight in front of you, and lift it slightly off the floor.

Keep your right leg straight and kick it upward as high as you can, letting out your breath and sucking in your stomach as the leg rises. From the top, lower the leg again, keeping it straight, but don't let it quite touch the floor.

Do your repetitions with
the right leg, then switch legs
and repeat the movement.

Repetitions:
10 to 20

Date & Reps   **Date & Reps**

155

Scissors Leg Raises

Lie on your back, your hands under your buttocks, palms down. Lock your legs out straight and lift them and your head slightly off the floor.

Cross the right foot over, left foot under in a scissors motion, then reverse and cross left over right.

Continue this scissors motion and, at the same time, lift your legs up as high as you can.

When you've raised your legs as far as you can, bring them slowly down, continuing the scissors motion.

This constitutes one repetition.

Repetitions:
10 to 20

Circular Leg Raises

Lie on your back, hands under your buttocks, palms down. Lock your legs out straight and lift them and your head slightly off the floor.

Keeping your legs straight, raise them as high as you can. At this point, instead of lowering them straight down, open them out as far apart as you can and bring them down in a wide curve. When you have almost reached the floor, bring them together from their split angle and raise them together to begin the next repetition.

Repetitions:
10 to 20

159

Super Crunches

Lie on your back. Keep your legs straight and lift them until they are pointing at the ceiling.

If you have trouble holding this position, you can lean your legs against a wall for support, or have a workout partner help hold them in place.

Keeping your legs stationary, raise your head and torso and try to touch your feet with your hands. At this point, lower yourself again, but don't let your head rest on the floor.

Repetitions:
10 to 20

Date & Reps	Date & Reps

PART VI
IMPROVISATIONAL TRAINING

On the Road

Jet lag. Unfamiliar surroundings and climate. Long hours, the tedium and fatigue of traveling. None of these things is particularly conducive to making you feel like training.

But these are just the sorts of circumstances that make training and conditioning your body all the more important. Travel, fatigue and tension drain the body of physical energy and, what can be even more important, take the edge off your mental faculties. Whether you are traveling for business reasons, or just for pleasure, it doesn't make any sense to arrive in a state that prevents you from getting the most out of your trip.

That is why I am just as careful to do some sort of workout on the road as I am at home. Whether I am getting ready to sit down to a business conference, appear on a television talk show or enjoy a weekend in the Bahamas, I want to be sure I am at 100 percent both physically and mentally. But staying in shape when you don't have access to equipment or much time to spend on workouts requires some thought and imagination. Over the years, I've worked out my own approach, and I'd like to share it with you.

Stretching and Abdominals

Your traveling workouts can be based to a large extent on what you already have learned. For one thing, your stretching and abdominal routines can be done just as easily in a hotel room as they can when you are at home. However, all the stresses and demands that traveling puts on your body require, I believe, certain variations in the way you train:

(1) *Take more time with your stretching.* Sitting all day on planes, trains or buses, the physical inactivity of conferences and meetings, or just being constantly in unfamiliar surroundings all tend to create stiff, tense and tight muscles. So it pays to start out slowly and carefully when you stretch out your body, and to take sufficient time to be sure you promote full physical relaxation and release of mental tensions.

(2) *Stretch and train abs twice a day.* A few minutes of exercise in the morning is a great way to set yourself up for the demands you will face during the day, and a short workout in the evening does wonders for ridding yourself of the stress and tensions you've accumulated since morning. So if this means getting up a few minutes early or making some small adjustments in your schedule, I really think that the benefits of both morning and evening stretching and ab training are well worth the effort.

Aerobic Training

Keeping your cardiovascular system in shape when you are traveling can be very difficult. Sitting around doesn't put much demand on the heart and lungs. But even on the road, aerobic training is not impossible. Here are a few suggestions:

(1) *Walk instead of ride.* Except for those long miles changing planes in a major airport always seems to involve, most traveling involves a lot of sitting down, and the antidote to this is to stay on your feet whenever you can. So if you're due at a meeting or restaurant a few blocks away, try walking there instead of calling a cab or taking the bus. When you take a break, spend it taking a walk around the block instead of sitting down to a cup of coffee or a drink. And when you walk, don't just amble along at a leisurely pace—the faster you walk, the more cardiovascular benefit you receive.

(2) *Use stairs when you can.* Elevators are easier, but if what you are after is exercise, then look for stairs you can use whenever you can spare the time.

(3) *Look for opportunities to run or swim.* It isn't unusual to see runners in jogging suits even in places like mid-town Manhattan. But in many cities, New York included, there are great places to run. So carry your running gear with you whenever you travel, and use it at every opportunity. Also, if you find a hotel or nearby facility with a swimming pool, jump in for a few laps. It doesn't take much time, but I have found that just a few minutes of this kind of high-repetition exercise can totally change my mood and vastly improve my feeling of well-being. It will work for you, as well.

(4) *Add some aerobic movements to your training.* When you are training with weights, the demands of the routine provide cardiovascular benefits as well as strengthening and conditioning your muscles. But on the road, when you aren't able to pursue weight training, you can compensate somewhat by doing some additional high-repetition exercises, or additional sets of the exercises you are already familiar with, to help develop and maintain your aerobic capacity.

Cardiovascular Training

The warm-up movements you have already mastered:

Standing Twists
Bent-Over Twists
Windmills
High Knees
Jumping Lunges

are fantastic for your cardiovascular conditioning.

But there are other movements you can include as well. In fact, almost any of the standard calisthenic exercises that most of us are familiar with can work to promote aerobic development as long as they are done in a rapid, demanding manner, and not too much time is taken to rest. For example:

Jumping Jacks: In this traditional exercise movement, stand with your feet together, arms at your side. With a jumping motion, spread your feet wide and simultaneously lift your arms out to each side and, in a wide arc, bring them together over your head as high as you can.

To return to the starting position, jump again, bringing your feet back together, while sweeping your arms out and down and back to your sides at the same time. **Repetitions:** *20*

More Aerobic Training

Anything that gets you breathing hard and raises your pulse rate constitutes a good cardiovascular exercise, but some types of movement accomplish this more effectively than others. In general, those movements in which you have to move your entire body weight are the best. In this category are Running, which takes a lot of space, and High Knees, which takes

My friend Jon Jon Park, son of former Mr. Universe Reg Park, faces the same problem I face—how to stay in shape while traveling. A competitive swimmer and swimming coach, he takes along a variety of portable exercise devices in his luggage whenever he travels from his home in South Africa. This enables Jon Jon to stay in super shape throughout the whole year no matter how much traveling he has to do.

little. But there are a couple of other variations that I have found invaluable to keep in shape while traveling.

Running the Steps: If you are in a multi-story hotel, going quickly up a few flights of stairs and then back down is highly demanding on the cardio-vascular system and good for developing the legs, as well. Incidentally, you don't have to run; you can get the same effect walking fast.

Jumping Rope: A jump rope is a piece of equipment that fits easily into any suitcase, and when you jump rope you get the benefits of running while developing your calves and physical coordination as well. But learn to do this movement correctly. Don't swing your arms in big circles. Instead, keep your hands close to the body and spin the rope with just a slight movement of the wrists. As you get your timing down, you will find you need not jump very high, and you can begin to experiment with heel-and-toe movements and other variations demanding more coordination.

Running in Place: High Knees is a good variation of running in place, but there are others. Sometimes you may find this exercise hard on your knees or ankles. The solution is to run in place on a chair or sofa cushion placed on the floor, or even doing this movement standing on the bed. Remember, all you are after is boosting up your resting pulse rate and keeping it up for a period of time.

Escalating the Intensity

Your cardiovascular system is adaptive, just like your muscles. When you start getting into shape, you may well find that a mere 20 repetitions of these aerobic exercises will hardly get you out of breath at all.

If all you are doing is warming up for weight training, this is no problem. If you are looking for further aerobic development, however, you are going to have to work for more intensity.

This means going beyond 20 repetitions of these exercises, and cutting down your rest periods as close to zero as you can. It is another case of progressive resistance—you have to keep making more demands if you want to continue to see results.

Improvisational Resistance Training

Obviously, most of us do not have dumbbells and barbells available when we travel, and we often don't have much time to devote to training, either. However, if you want to keep the gains you have accomplished with your weight training, you are going to have to continue to contract your muscles against resistance, even when you are away from home.

One way to accomplish this is with calisthenics, using the weight of your own body to provide resistance so that you can maintain whatever muscular strength and hypertrophy you have achieved.

Again, the name of the game is improvisation. You may eventually develop a program that suits your individual needs but is totally unlike the one I use.

In the meantime, I recommend a simple circuit of 8 exercises which can be done no matter where you happen to be:

Between-Chair Push-ups
Doorknob Pull-ups
Deep Knee Bends
Lunges

One-Legged Calf Raises
Chin-ups
Leg Raises
Knee-Elbow Touches

3 circuits of these exercises, I believe, will give you the minimum benefit with the least expenditure of time. If you want to do more—fine. But do at least this much.

IMPROVISATIONAL RESISTANCE TRAINING

Between-Chair Push-ups

Push-ups are like upside-down Bench Presses, and primarily work the pectoral muscles. However, doing Push-ups between two chairs allows you to lower yourself farther toward the floor, stretch the muscles of the chest, and work them over a greater range of motion.

The Exercise
Place two chairs a few feet apart just less than a body-length from the bed. Assume a Push-up position, one hand on each chair, your feet on the bed.

Keeping your back and legs straight, lower yourself slowly down between the chairs as far as you can go. From this position, push yourself back up until you return to the starting position.

In this movement, the farther apart you position the chairs, the more difficult the exercise. However, be certain that the chairs don't slide out from under you as you are doing the exercise.

Repetitions:
10

IMPROVISATIONAL RESISTANCE TRAINING

Doorknob Pull-ups

This is a rowing motion that works the lats and the upper back as well as the biceps.

The Exercise
Stand with your feet on either side of a door and grasp the doorknobs with a firm grip. Bending your knees, sink down and back until your arms are fully extended, thighs about parallel to the floor.

From here, pull yourself back up to the starting position, squeezing the muscles of your back together so that they work through the maximum possible range of motion.

Repetitions:
20

IMPROVISATIONAL RESISTANCE TRAINING

Deep Knee Bends

This exercise is a method of doing Squats without any extra weight held across your shoulders. However, your own body weight is enough to make the muscles of the thighs really get a good workout.

The Exercise

Place your hands on your hips and stand with your feet comfortably apart. Bending your knees and keeping your back straight, head up, lower yourself until your thighs are parallel to the floor.

From here, straighten your legs and bring yourself back up to the starting position.

Repetitions:
20

IMPROVISATIONAL RESISTANCE TRAINING

Lunges

Lunges develop the quadriceps (the front of the thighs).

The Exercise

Stand with your feet together, hands on your hips. Step forward with your left foot, bend your left knee and lower yourself toward the floor. Your back should be kept straight. Continue down until your right knee almost touches the floor, then push back up to the starting position.

Repeat the movement stepping forward with the right foot, then continue to alternate left and right.

Repetitions:
10 with each leg

IMPROVISATIONAL RESISTANCE TRAINING

One-Legged Calf Raises

Calf Raises train the calf muscles of the lower leg.

The Exercise
Place the toes of one foot on a stair, block or telephone book, and hold onto something for balance and support. Hook your other foot behind your leg.

Lower yourself as far as you can until the heel of your supporting foot approaches or just brushes the floor. From here, raise back up and as high onto the toes as you can. Make sure you go through the full range of motion possible on each repetition.

Do your repetitions with one leg, then switch and do the same number with the other.

Repetitions:
At least 20 with each leg

IMPROVISATIONAL RESISTANCE TRAINING

Chin-ups

To do this movement on the road, you will need a portable chinning bar, which is a piece of equipment that many people find possible to carry with them when they travel.

Chinning yourself is a tremendous exercise for working the muscles of the back and arms, and has a good deal of aerobic benefit as well.

The Exercise

Fasten your chinning bar inside a door frame, making sure that the bar is secure and that the door structure is strong enough to bear your weight.

Grasp the bar so that your palms are turned to face you, hands slightly more than shoulder-width apart. Lift your feet off the floor, curl them up behind you, and let yourself hang at arm's length beneath the bar.

Pull yourself up until your chin is just above the bar, hold this position for a moment, then lower yourself slowly back to the starting position.

I recommend 20 repetitions. If you find you are able to do only a few at a time, do these, stop and rest, and then do some more until you have done a total of 20.

Leg Raises

A basic exercise for the abdominals, and one you should include in your program even if you are doing little else for the mid-section.

The Exercise

Lie on your back on the floor (or on a bed, if space is a problem) and put your hands, palms down, under your buttocks for support.

Raise your legs slowly up as high as you can, then lower them once more, not letting them touch at the bottom of the movement.

The straighter you keep your legs, the more difficult the exercise; the more you bend your knees, the easier it becomes.

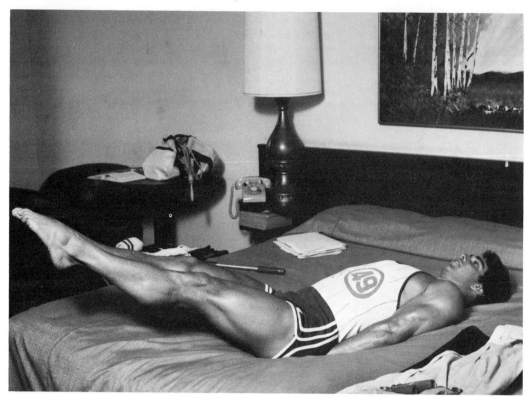

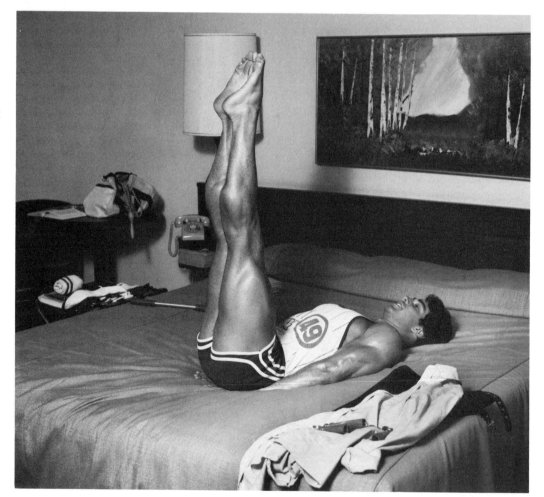

Repetitions:
20

Knee-Elbow Touches

Because of the twisting
motion involved, this exercise
not only works the abdominal
muscles, but the other muscles of the torso as well.

The Exercise

Lie on your back, your hands
behind your head. Keeping
your right leg straight, bend
your left knee and bring it up
as far toward your head as
possible. At the same time,
lift and turn your upper body,
bringing your right elbow as
close to the knee as you can.

Straighten your leg and
lower your upper body.
Repeat the movement, this
time bringing up the right
knee and trying to touch it
with your left elbow.

Repetitions:
10 to each side

PART VII
TEENAGE TRAINING

Growing Up Strong

When I was a kid, I wanted to be the best soccer player in the world. And I trained really hard, running back and forth across the stadium, developing flexibility and coordination and practicing the skills important to mastering soccer. Along the way I took up training with weights, and that led to my discovering bodybuilding and making it my life.

That was when I was around 15 years old, and my body had begun to mature enough so that it could bear up under moderately heavy resistance exercise. If I had tried to train earlier than that, it would not have been good for me. And I have seen many youngsters who, even at 16 or 17, are not really ready for heavy training.

Preteens and Young Teenagers

Parents and young would-be bodybuilders ask me all the time how early a kid should take up bodybuilding. Individuals differ so much, that all I can do is to give some general guidelines:

(1) Pre-teens should *not* train with weights. At that age, I recommend a lot of calesthenics, training with the weight of the body alone, and developing the cardiovascular system through activities like running, bicycling and swimming.

(2) Young teenagers are at an age where some resistance training is beneficial, but they should go for high reps instead of heavy weights. Unfortunately, the muscles mature before the bones do, and it is easy to lift too much weight for your physical structure to support. However, on the plus side, the body at that age is so prone to growth that it doesn't take much resistance training to stimulate an accumulation of muscle mass.

(3) When the body is ready, which may be as early as 14 for some young men or as late as 18 or 19 for others, training with heavier weights can be attempted to produce large gains of strength and muscle mass.

Teenage Physiology

Even if you tried, it would be impossible to build a lot of mass at age 12 or 13. The body at that age is burning up so much energy in spurts of growth that there is little left over to devote to building muscle mass. At the age of puberty, the body begins to produce an abundance of male hormones, and these will eventually allow the muscles to get a lot bigger. But it is important to let the body get its growth first.

In a mature man, the ends of bones are as hard and tough as the rest of the bones, but this is not true of a teenager. In a youngster, the muscles may be strong and the body apparently mature, but the ends of the bones are still soft and can be damaged by lifting too heavy a weight.

But whether you are 9, 13, 16 or whatever, your body will respond to physical training. The trick is to give it the right kind.

Teenage Training

Teenagers require the same kinds of cardiovascular and flexibility conditioning that adults do. The only difference is that, being young, they will tend to respond faster and better to this kind of training than older people. However, when it comes to resistance training, there should be quite a difference:

(1) *High-reps, low-weight.* A young man can do all the same exercises, but his aim should be different. Instead of going for 10 or 12 reps a set, I would recommend trying to do at least 25 repetitions at a time. I know one young wrestler who won his state championship by doing 100 repetitions of each movement in as short a time as possible, which gave him both strength and tremendous endurance.

(2) *Train as fast as possible.* Go through each of your sets at a good pace, and then get through as many sets as you can without stopping. Go right from one exercise to another. Force your body to cope with this intensity, and you will be pleased and proud of the results.

(3) *Train the whole body.* This is true for everyone, but the young guys I know are especially prone to make this mistake: They want big arms or a big chest, and they neglect the other parts of the body. The right kind of development is all-around development, especially if you ever want to go on to be a competition bodybuilder.

(4) *Don't neglect nutrition.* Because they are growing so rapidly, and burning up a lot of calories, a lot of teenage boys can get away with eating terrible diets. The problem is that if you don't give the body the basic nutrients it needs you will not grow up as big and strong as your genetic potential is patterned for, and you may very well suffer from deficiencies acquired at this time for the rest of your life. Your body needs protein, complex carbohydrate, vitamins and minerals, as much or more as it will when you are older. So don't make the mistake of training to become big and strong without giving the body the fuel it requires to grow the way you want it to.

(5) *Develop in every way you can.* Bodybuilders in their twenties may want to specialize and devote most of their energies to weight training, but you should be working to develop *all* of your physical talents, the way I did when I was training for soccer. Even if you are not interested in becoming a first-rate athlete, remember that your body is the vehicle that is going to carry you through life, and it's the only one you will ever have. Your future health and well-being may well depend upon the foundation of physical fitness you lay down now—and I don't mean physical conditioning *instead* of learning and education, I mean *in addition to.* Whatever your goals in life, if you develop both mind and body you have just that much of an edge toward achieving them.

Playing at Fitness

Working at something can often be unpleasant, and therefore it requires a lot of discipline. Playing, on the other hand, is fun and not difficult at all. Playing at fitness is called sport or athletics, and it can be the most fun of all.

Nowadays, so much sport for youngsters is so organized and competitive that some kids don't find it fun at all. But it isn't necessary to engage in sport on that level to get the physical and psychological benefits of athletic play. If you are the competitive type and you really get off on highly structured competition, be my guest. If you aren't, don't force yourself. There are other alternatives.

Every athletic skill is to some degree unique. A great baseball player may or may not be good at football, much less at skiing. As the television show "Superstars" has demonstrated, you can be a heck of an athlete and still make a fool of yourself if you try to compete in a sport for which you've had no training.

Not everybody is good at everything, but the more kinds of sports you get involved in the more of your physical potential will be realized. Running, jumping, throwing, catching, and other physical skills are best learned by trying the sports in which they play an important part. Have fun while you are learning. It will get more like work soon enough without your rushing it.

If you're a teenager, you can use all of the exercises in this book as part of your personal training program. However, here is a list of some of the exercises that I think are especially valuable to somebody your age:

1. Running

Running is probably the best overall conditioning exercise for your heart, lungs, circulatory system and legs. You can hardly do enough, if you take the trouble to build up your endurance slowly. Other good aerobic exercises include bicycle riding, swimming, jumping rope and the like.

2. Running Steps

Moving your body weight across the ground is great exercise; having to lift it up a flight of stairs and then running back down is even better. Running Steps is a first-rate exercise for everyone, but especially for serious athletes.

3. Push-ups

Primarily for the chest, but
for the deltoids and triceps as
well.

4. Close-Grip Push-ups

A Push-up variation that puts most of the training effort on the triceps to build up arm strength and endurance.

5. Chin-ups

A great back exercise. Palms turned away is a more difficult version than palms turned toward you. And the more you spread your hands apart, the harder it is to do a Chin-up.

6. Calf Raises

Do them one leg at a time, and be sure to drop as low as you can, and raise up just as high as you can on your toes. Keep it up until they really burn.

7. Dips

Raise yourself up on some parallel bars and lock out your arms, then dip down as far as you can in between them. When you lean forward during this movement you tend to use more chest; staying more upright you put stress primarily on the triceps.

8. Lunges

Good for building the legs, and also a good warm-up before playing sports. If you take a slightly longer than normal stride you will stretch out the muscles of the inner leg and groin.

The preceding exercises rely on your own body weight. For the following, you will need a pair of dumbbells.

9. Shoulder Press

Stand upright, holding a dumbbell in each hand at shoulder height, palms facing toward you. Lift the dumbbells simultaneously straight up as far as you can, locking out your elbows. Lower them again deliberately, keeping them under control, back to the starting position.

10. Laterals

Stand upright, a dumbbell in each hand at arm's length beside you, palms turned in toward the body. Keeping your arms straight, raise the dumbbells up and out to the side in as wide an arc as possible until they reach a level about even with the top of your head. Keep your palms turned toward the floor during this movement. At the top, lower the weights deliberately in the same arc and return to the starting position.

11. Triceps Extensions

Take a dumbbell in one hand, hold it at arm's length over your head, the elbow close to the ear. Lower the dumbbell slowly down behind your head as far as you can, feeling the stretch in the triceps (back of the arm) but not letting the elbow move away from the ear. Raise the dumbbell back to the starting position, then repeat the exercise using the other arm.

12. Dumbbell Curls

Stand upright, a dumbbell in each hand held at arm's length beside you. Turn your wrists so that your palms and the inside of the forearms face forward. Keeping your elbows anchored at your side, raise the weights forward and up as far as you can, feeling a "cramping" of the biceps at the top of the movement. Lower the weights deliberately through the same arc and return to the starting position. Make sure your arms are fully stretched at the bottom and fully contracted at the top.

13. Squats

Stand upright, a dumbbell in each hand held at arm's length beside you. Keeping your back straight and your head up, bend your knees and lower your body, letting heels lift off the floor as necessary, until your thighs are about parallel to the floor. Straighten your legs and push your body back up to the starting position.

14. Lunges with Dumbbells

Stand upright, a dumbbell in each hand held at arm's length beside you. Step forward with one leg, bend your knees, and lower your body so that the knee of the trailing leg just brushes the floor. Push back up and bring your feet together in the starting position, and repeat the movement with the other leg. The longer your stride as you step forward, the more difficult the exercise; the shorter, the easier.

15. Bent-Over Rows

Take a dumbbell in each hand. Bend your knees slightly, bend forward from the waist until your upper body is about parallel to the floor. Let your arms and the weights hang directly down from your shoulders, palms facing each other. Without lifting up your body at all, raise the weights slowly as close to your shoulders as you can. Lower them again deliberately to arm's length, feeling the stretch in your lats (upper back).

BIDING YOUR TIME
The body has its own time-table of growth and development and you can't rush it. The way you make progress is by understanding what your body is telling you, and going along with its needs. For a teenager, this means training hard, developing as many physical skills as necessary, eating right, but avoiding the use of potentially harmful heavy weights.

PART VIII
COMPETITION
BODYBUILDING
Taking the Next Step

It is tough to predict who will actually decide to become a competition bodybuilder. Some kids know that competition is for them from the very first time they pick up a weight. Others train for a number of years before the competition bug bites them.

Most people take up training with weights in order to shape up their bodies and become physically fit and healthy. Out of this group, there will always be some who will discover a deeper and more intense interest. They will decide that getting a lot bigger and stronger is a goal that really turns them on. Of these, a smaller percentage will actually commit themselves to the discipline of training for high-level competition bodybuilding.

Bodybuilding on this level is a unique activity, virtually a way of life. It involves developing unusual amounts of muscle mass, sculpting all the shapes, planes, angles and contours of the body by a variety of carefully selected exercises, and dieting away as much body fat as possible so that this development become visible.

One reason why certain people get interested in bodybuilding is simply because they are good at it. They start training with weights and suddenly their bodies begin to respond and develop rapidly. Not everybody has this physical capacity, just as not everybody can run a 9.1 hundred-yard dash or run a sub-four-minute mile, no matter how much or how hard he trains.

My friend Franco Columbu, himself a Mr. Universe and Mr. Olympia, is a good example. When he first came into the gym he was a 130-pound boxer who had no real interest in hard-core bodybuilding. But

within a few weeks he discovered he had a talent for lifting enormous amounts of weight, and he began to train harder. Within a few years Franco was recognized as, pound for pound, one of the strongest men in the world, and his body had developed to the point where he has won a place for himself as one of the top bodybuilders of all time.

This kind of discovery can happen to somebody after a month, a year or even five years of training. It can develop as a desire to become a competitive powerlifter or a bodybuilder. However, once the decision is made, a whole other attitude toward training is called for. Your workouts have to become the center of your life, not just another of several types of activity. You need dedication, and you have to be prepared to make sacrifices. I have seen that even those people who find that they have the physical talent it takes to be a bodybuilder sometimes don't have the attributes of character and personality that allow them to persevere in this difficult undertaking. The ones who do are the stars you see in the pages of *Muscle and Fitness* magazine or winning bodybuilding events on "The CBS Sports Spectacular," NBC's "Sportsworld" and ABC's "Wide World of Sports."

Assessing Your Potential

"If wishes were horses then beggars would ride," and if everyone who ever wanted to be a champion bodybuilder could achieve that goal, we'd have champions coming out of our ears. Obviously, since we don't, not everyone has the potential to succeed in competition bodybuilding.

But assessing potential in bodybuilding is more difficult than in practically any other sport. For example, when I first saw pictures of Frank Zane years ago I could never have believed he would develop into the champion he is today. And when Franco Columbu first came into the gym, nobody thought he had a chance to succeed as a bodybuilder. His arms, legs and torso were too short; his proportions seemed totally unsuited to developing into an aesthetically outstanding physique.

The fact that both Frank and Franco did succeed demonstrates that early assessments of potential in bodybuilding can be way off the mark. Getting to the top in any sport is difficult, and getting there without an overabundance of natural potential makes it even tougher. But not impossible. It just increases the risk, stacks the odds more against you. But odds are just statistics and few really serious competitors let numbers get in the way of winning.

If you look in the mirror and see wide shoulders, a narrow waist, long arms and legs, and you have the mental dedication and motivation to train harder than anyone else, then the odds shift more in your favor. If you're someone like Franco with short arms, legs and torso, the risk you are taking in spending five years or so training for competition is that much greater. You have to decide if it's worth it.

Franco went all out training his legs to develop a shape that would draw attention away from their shortness; in addition, he used high-cut posing trunks to further create the illusion of longer legs. He developed his lats so that they swept way down toward his waist to improve the look of his upper body. Finally, he created such a muscular physique that any deficiencies still evident just didn't seem to matter.

I never had a particularly narrow waist, but I was so big that I was able to pile on size in the chest, lats and delts so that, visually, everything fitted together. After all, the judges don't go running around with a tape measure.

But I should point out that I didn't just wake up one morning and decide I was going to be a bodybuilder. I began weight training to be a better soccer player, and I was an avid swimmer and skier as well. My body responded so well to my gym workouts that I soon fell in love with bodybuilding. By trying lots of different things, I discovered the one that meant the most to me, and even when I was 16 years old and had been training only a year, you could already see my physique taking on the lines that made me a champion.

I think it makes sense for you to examine other sports along with bodybuilding to find out just where your heart lies. Physically, you may be equally suited to bodybuilding, powerlifting and discus throwing, for example, but you might love one and only like the others. At a certain level, success is determined by mental factors, by dedication and motivation, and these things can't be faked. You either really care, or you don't. You are either hungry, or not.

So look around awhile before you settle. Many who are second-rate at one sport go on to be champions in another. Try a lot of things, and then if you decide that you are willing to give 100% dedication to bodybuilding, go to it and give it all you've got!

Meanwhile, I recommend that you continue to develop the rest of your life as well. Don't give up on your education, for instance. All during my own career, even while I was winning my six Mr. Olympia titles, I continued to take college courses toward earning a university degree. Believe me, this effort has allowed me to take much greater advantage of the opportunities that being a champion opened up to me. In these modern times, bodybuilding is a lot more complicated than just pumping up in the gym, and you have to be ready to deal with all sorts of problems in order to fully succeed.

Competition Training

The training a competition bodybuilder undergoes involves using most of the same exercises that are part of a fitness training program. But the training has to become harder, longer and more intense. And it has to be tailored to the individual's own physique, taking into account all his unique strengths and weaknesses.

The first task is to develop sufficient muscle mass. You need quantity. Once you've gotten this, you need to train for proportion, symmetry, balance and muscular definition—in other words, quality. Along with this, your diet becomes of paramount importance. You need to eat to grow, but also learn to burn off body fat to reveal the lines of your physique. Finally, once you have created the kind of physique you desire, you must learn to pose and to present yourself in a dramatic, dynamic and effective manner.

If I were to try and categorize what is necessary in developing workouts to build a championship physique, I would advise young bodybuilders to concentrate on the following areas:

(1) Expanding their training routines.
(2) Learning to structure their training routines.
(3) Developing championship-level intensity.

(4) Eating to win.

(5) Mastering presentation.

Competition Training Routines

In the beginning, I always advise young bodybuilders to stick to the basics and try to build as strong and fundamental a physical structure as they can. In other words: stick to a few exercises, and work at them as hard as you can.

After you have built your basic structure, then comes the time for adding lots of additional exercises to fill out and complete your physical development. The difference between weightlifters and bodybuilders is that the latter train every single muscle in their bodies from every angle possible to get the maximum of overall development, rather than sticking to a few basic lifts.

Once you have passed the beginner stage, you can begin to add new exercises to your routines. As you become more knowledgeable about bodybuilding, you will no doubt develop your own preferences.

This is the training schedule I used for the Mr. Olympia contest:

Sets and Reps

You commonly hear that high-rep sets produce definition, while low-rep sets create muscle mass. This is only partially true. The idea, in all cases, is to try and make your body fire off as many muscle fibers as possible so that you get the maximum muscle contraction. This is what builds both muscle and strength.

It takes a lot of concentration to get maximum intensity with just a few reps. It makes more sense to work with a fairly heavy weight and go for 8 or 10 reps, figuring that as you get toward the last reps and your muscles get tired they will have to call upon additional muscle fibers to keep the weight moving.

I like to do a series of five sets, progressively increasing the weight.

Set 1: 15 reps with light weight

Set 2: 10 reps with heavier weight

Set 3: 10 reps with heavier weight

Set 4: 8 reps with heavier weight

Set 5: 6 reps with very heavy weight

All in all, I recommend at least 20 sets total for most body parts, enough so that you are able to work all the various muscles, angles and contours, and at least 15 to 16 sets for the biceps and the same for the triceps (one of the simple muscle groups).

If you have difficulty building mass, work your program starting with 12 reps instead of 15 and go down to 4 instead of 6, which will allow you to lift heavier weights. And there is nothing to stop you from setting one session a week aside for doing nothing but 3- to 6-rep power moves, something that even Mr. Olympia winner Frank Zane still does from time to time.

Split Routines

In the old days, bodybuilders worked their entire bodies three times a week. The more modern method is the "split routine." This means breaking up your body part workouts and concentrating on different parts of the body different days. An example of that would be:

Mon.	Tues.	Wed.
Shoulders	Back	Legs
Arms	Chest	

Thurs.	Fri.	Sat.	Sun.
Shoulders	Back	Legs	Off
Arms	Chest		

You can also set up a five-day-a-week schedule instead of six, or even one which allows you to train only four days. The trick is to find what your own personal preference is for balancing off the training/rest cycle.

Double Split Routines

This is an advanced method of organizing workouts that is followed by the majority of top bodybuilders nowadays. Training this way, you not only break up your training so that you work certain body parts certain days of the week, but you also break up your daily training into two separate sessions. An example would be coming into the gym in the morning and doing a hard shoulder and calf training routine, then coming back in the evening, rested and refreshed, and bombing your back and abs.

You can train intensely only for a limited period of time, just as you can sprint at top speed only for a limited distance. Therefore, breaking up your training into two sessions per day allows you to attack each session with greater intensity than would be possible if you tried to do them both together.

Intensity

I've used the word "intensity" several times and I'd like to explain further what it means. Intensity is the key to success in bodybuilding. It means working as close as possible to 100 percent of your capacity, because anything less is not going to force your muscles to develop as fast as they can. You can't pace yourself. You have to get in there and dig. There is a

formula which states that you can work hard or work long but not both—but the trick to bodybuilding training is to work as hard as you can for as long as you can.

If you do 20 sets of chest in an hour, and then do the same number of sets with the same weight in 45 minutes in your next session, although you have not lifted more weight you have done more work. You can shock the body with weight, surprise it by compressing time, and either way you will cause it to grow better.

Ultimately, intensity is mental. It means concentrating on what you are doing, getting the most from each rep and each set, never cheating to make the lift easier, and working just as hard when you lower the weights as when you raise them.

Up to a point, the body does the work, and then the mind takes over. To cross the limits set up by the inhibitions built into the physical organism to protect it from injury due to too much stress, you have to develop the right mental outlook. That's how you create intensity, and that's what it takes to make a champion.

In my own case, I find that the goal I am training for almost automatically affects my level of intensity. For instance, if I'm training just for fitness, I'll go into the gym and have no reason at all to do 15 sets for a body part instead of 10. But the moment I were to decide to go back into competition, my mind and body would respond and I would do the 15 sets or even 20 without giving it any thought. The mind, as I say, ultimately controls the body and delivers that ultimate level of intensity.

The Bodybuilding Environment

A few good bodybuilders are able to train at home or in their garages, but for most the key to success is training in the right kind of gym. You don't necessarily have to come out to California and train at World Gym or Gold's Gym, but you do have to find a place where there is enough intensity so that unusual effort is considered normal. If you can do a 250-pound Bench Press and nobody around you can do any better, you are going to have trouble progressing to 300 pounds. But if there are some bodybuilders pressing 500 pounds right beside you, you are not going to remain satisfied with your own efforts for long.

You need a gym with both the right kind of facilities and the right atmosphere. You have to be able to concentrate on what you're doing, and some gyms allow this, while others discourage it. If you can find the right kind of training partner, so much the better. When you are aiming at 100 percent intensity in your workouts, you need somebody to kick you in the behind from time to time as well as to praise you and give you encouragement when you finally get it right.

Along with this physical environment, you need the right kind of mental environment, too. I remember I used to increase my motivation by hanging up photos around my room of bodybuilders like Reg Park and Bill Pearl, huge guys whom I wanted to emulate. And I also went to see a lot of motivational films, sometimes totally unrelated to bodybuilding. I would use the inspiration of great heroes and those who conquered against great odds to make me work even harder for my own success.

I loved to read biographies of those who came

from out of nowhere and made a big success, because I, also, wanted to be a big success, a world champion. I'd listen to inspirational music, everything from symphonies to disco music, whatever drove me to work past my previous limits. I know that when the film *Rocky* first came out, whenever the theme was played in the gym suddenly everyone felt inspired to train harder.

Nowadays, there are my books and articles as well as those of other bodybuilders like Franco Columbu to help provide you with an endless source of motivation. And there are lots of good contests to provide you with the inspiration of seeing others up on stage where you would like to be, and helping you to keep your own personal goals that much more firmly in mind.

Eating to Win

Bodybuilders get impatient. They train as hard as they can, but the body develops at its own pace. So everyone is always looking for an edge, something that will speed up their progress by even a tiny little bit. Like a lot of other athletes, bodybuilders often turn to diet and nutrition to give them that edge.

When I was first starting out, I knew nothing about diet and nutrition. Growing up in Austria, I had no idea of what things like TV dinners were. My mother always served me a varied diet that included fresh vegetables and fruit, and so I grew up strong and well-nourished.

That, it turns out, is the basis of the best kind of diet for maximizing bodybuilding development. Kids nowadays, raised on so much processed and convenience food, tend to go overboard when they dis-

Chest:

Wide-Grip Bench Press

Incline Bench Press 45°

Dumbbell Flys

Dips on parallel bar

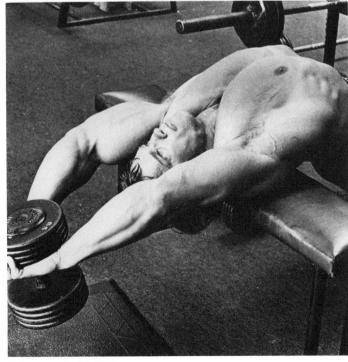

Pullovers with dumbbell

Cable Flys

Back:

Wide-Grip Chin-ups

Rowing on lat machine, narrow grip

Bent-Over Rowing with T-bar

Pull-downs on lat machine, narrow grip

Barbell Rowing, wide grip

Thighs:

Squats

Leg Extensions

Leg Curl

Leg Press

Calves:

Calf Raises standing

Calf Raises seated

Waist:

Leg Raises

Bent-Over Twist

Crunches

Shoulders:

Military Press

Laterals on bench

Cable Laterals seated

Front Laterals with dumbbell

Cable Laterals standing

Triceps:

Triceps Push-down on machine

Single Arm Dumbbell Extension

Dip behind the back

Triceps Extension seated

Seated Arm Triceps Kick-Back

Biceps:

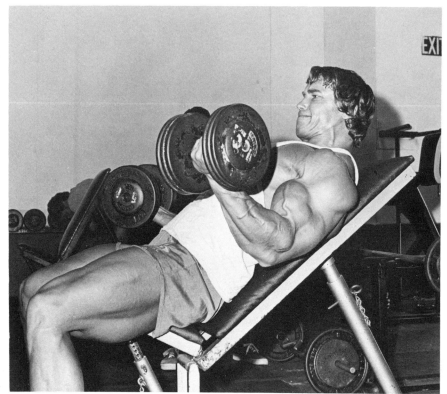

Barbell Curl

Seated Incline Curl

Dumbbell Curl standing

Bench Curl with bar

Forearms:

Wrist Curl

Calves:

Calf Raises seated

Reverse Curl

Calf Raises standing

Waist:

Leg Raises

Twist with stick

Crunches

cover bodybuilding and eat diets consisting of 50 to 70% protein, something I believe to be totally unnecessary.

It is hard for me to convince them that what they ought to be eating is a basic, balanced diet, just like the one they were taught about back in health education class in school. I know they want something more exotic, but I can't help the way things are. That kind of balanced diet is necessary to provide the body with all of the essential nutrients it requires for the difficult and demanding training that bodybuilding involves.

Here is my formula for basic good eating:

(1) Eat about 1 gram of protein for every 2 pounds of body weight.

(2) Eat no less than 60 and no more than 100 grams of carbohydrate per day.

(3) Limit your fat intake.

(4) Take a limited amount of vitamin and mineral supplementation just for insurance.

(5) If you want to gain or lose weight, vary your caloric intake—and that variation should be mostly in carbohydrates, in the form of vegetables, potatoes and fruit.

Earlier in my career, I believed that a bodybuilder needed to eat as much as 200 grams of protein a day in order to develop the maximum muscle mass. Since then, my research has shown me that bodybuilders do need more protein than the average person, but probably no more than around 100 grams, and certainly no more than 150. This gives enough protein for muscle-building, without adding any unnecessary calories to the diet. Non-bodybuilders, on the other hand, can easily get by on no more than 1 gram of protein for every kilo (2.2 pounds) of body weight.

The basic difference between a bodybuilding diet and that of other athletes or the average person is the degree of leanness a bodybuilder has to achieve in order to appear really cut-up and defined on stage. This is difficult because heavy weight training, by its nature, doesn't burn up as many calories as many other athletic activities. And the hardest part of this is to achieve just the look you want, to "peak" right on time for a contest, because you can't hold this state for more than a couple of days at most. This takes a lot of experience and experimentation.

But one hint I can give is not to "bulk up," or let yourself put on a lot of extra fat weight during your training that will only have to be dieted off for the contest. Bodybuilders are apt to do this because being heavier makes them feel bigger, but this is an illusion—that extra weight is not working muscle and it does them no good whatsoever.

Both Franco and I used to approach a contest actually *under* our competition weights, and thus had to gain five pounds or so the final week. This meant we didn't have to restrict our diets too much, and we ended up feeling better and stronger, and looking a lot better. Bulking up, I believe, is a mistake, and now that there is a Grand Prix circuit of professional contests, which the pros have to be ready for week after week, the practice of becoming overweight and then dieting severely is getting to be a thing of the past.

But dieting for bodybuilding requires discipline. To keep your relative fat weight down, you simply can't eat as much as you would like. Even when you are getting enough nutrients, you may still feel deprived. One way to ease this is to take up some form of high-calorie workout in addition to your training in the gym. Remember, for every 100 calories you burn up running or riding a bicycle, that is another 100 calories you can add to your diet without gaining any weight.

But all that dieting is worth it. Thin is in, as far as bodybuilding is concerned. When you have two bodybuilders of equal development, it is the one with the cuts—the most definition—who is going to win. You just have to learn to do a lot of "push-aways," that is, away from the dinner table.

Here are a few more hints about good eating for bodybuilding:

(1) Eggs have good protein, but a lot of fat. Don't eat more than 3 a day.

(2) Meats like beef and pork contain high amounts of fat; substitute low-fat sources of protein like chicken and fish whenever you can.

(3) Desserts and food with processed sugar give you a lot of calories with little or no nutritional value; vegetables, on the other hand, like potatoes, broccoli, asparagus and the like contain complex carbohydrate, which is high in various kinds of essential nutrients.

(4) Fruit contains fructose, a sugar that is many times sweeter than processed sugar; however, there is very little of it present in fruit, so the calories are reasonable, and fruit also contains a number of important vitamins and minerals.

(5) Having a greater number of small meals per day is a better way to eat than having a few big ones.

(6) If it's been processed or in any way pre-prepared, chances are food has had extra sugar and salt added.

(7) Losing or gaining weight is a gradual process; trying to do it overnight is really hard on the body.

Presentation

The finest diamond in the world appears nothing more than a lump of stone until it is cut. No matter how beautiful a painting, it makes little impression if it is poorly framed and lit. And no matter how tremendous the development of your physique, you will not win contests until you master the art of presenting yourself on stage.

Bodybuilding is both a sport and an art form. It is a sport in that developing and shaping your physique requires an enormous amount of athletic activity training in the gym. But that physique must be shown off on stage in a series of dynamic, carefully controlled poses, and that makes bodybuilding a performing art as well.

When you step out in front of bodybuilding judges, everything about your appearance is taken into consideration:

(1) *Skin tone.* A bodybuilder should have clear, healthy skin. If he's white, he needs a good-looking tan as well.

(2) *Haircut.* Too much hair takes away from the apparent size of the neck, traps and shoulders. Too little, on some people, can take away from overall appearance.

(3) *Posing trunks.* Depending on your proportions, you may want trunks that are cut higher or lower on the hip, or with a higher or lower rise in the waist—whatever best suits your appearance. Solid colors are usually better than stripes or other variations, and quite often darker colors look better on whites, brighter tones on blacks.

(4) *General manner.* You are being watched every moment you are on stage, whether you are posing or not. You must appear confident without being arrogant, and you can never let down, allowing your abs to bulge out, for instance, without making a bad impression on the judges.

(5) *Posing.* The most critical, individual and creative aspect of presentation.

Learning to Pose

You can't practice posing too much. I always believed in flexing and posing whatever body parts I was training during any workout in the gym. If I trained arms, I would stop between sets and do some arm shots, studying myself in the mirror. Training legs or anything else, I would always take time to pose.

Posing this way is not vanity. It has two specific advantages. On the one hand, this constant flexing is itself a good form of training, helping to make the muscles hard and well-defined. On the other, it constantly shows you exactly how much development you have achieved or failed to achieve.

As great as your physique may appear at rest, it will primarily be judged as seen in poses. Therefore, what it looks like when you pose is the ultimate measure of your success. That is why I always assessed my physique by seeing what I looked like posing. Did I need more cuts in the upper back? Was I getting the right tie-in between pecs and delts? There is no way to tell without examining the body in each of the important poses, and that's why I felt I could never pose enough.

The Basic Posing Routine

In I.F.B.B. (International Federation of Bodybuilders —the dominant sanctioning body for international bodybuilding) and other contests, you are judged in four rounds.

During the pre-judging, you
(1) Stand relaxed, to be seen from all four sides;
(2) Do six mandatory poses;
(3) Do a short, individualized posing routine.
In the evening show, you are then called upon to come out and repeat your own posing routine, but, usually, the outcome of the contest is all but decided by the end of the pre-judging.

The six mandatory poses are:
(1) Front double-biceps & rear double-biceps
(2) Side chest shot from both sides
(3) Front lat spread and rear lat spread
The first thing you have to do is to master these poses. Begin by practicing in front of a mirror, then try doing the poses without watching yourself—after all, you won't have a mirror on stage. Have a friend watch you and help you correct your mistakes. As with any other athletic skill, posing requires constant coaching, since small errors can creep in to your routine and become exaggerated with time.

Individualized Posing

Beginning and intermediate bodybuilders should concentrate on learning the basic poses. But, to go on further in bodybuilding, you have to expand your posing routines and include movements that show off your physique to its best advantage, and take attention away from areas that are less than perfect.

It is amazing how many great bodybuilders were able to win contests doing nothing but a few, simple poses. But I have also seen times when competitors with inferior physiques were able to achieve victory purely on the basis of their posing routines and overall stage presence. All in all, the better you pose, the better your chances in a contest.

The basic rule to follow is that it's better to do a few poses well than a lot of poses badly. It takes time to develop a good, personal routine. You have to choose the poses that really suit your particular physique, that call attention to your strengths and distract from your weaknesses. You also have to learn to go from one pose to another in such an assured manner that you never stumble, hesitate or lose control.

I was going through some old photographs of myself recently and I was amazed that, at one time or another, I seem to have tried every pose in the book. I did Frank Zane poses and Sergio Oliva poses and a lot of others. Over a period of time, I was able to find out what really worked for me. I finally settled on a routine that included a lot of wide, sweeping movements to capitalize on my height and long proportions. My friend Franco, on the other hand, being short and compact, developed a style that stressed strong, Herculean poses that were more suited to his physique.

Posing Practice

Posing requires just as much attention as the rest of your training, if you are going to become good at presentation. All you need for this practice is a full-length mirror and plenty of light. Ed Corney, one of the best posers of all time, used to spend at least an hour a day in front of the mirror working on his routine, and that was in addition to the time spent in the gym doing a double-split workout.

An important part of posing is getting from one pose to another, and this is often harder than it looks. The idea is to take your time. If you can't do it slow, you can't do it. After you have full control of the movement, and you know exactly what you are doing and where you are going, then you can speed up to a normal pace.

Remember, when you actually enter a contest, and you are being pre-judged, you may be forced to hit certain poses over and over for a matter of hours. If you haven't practiced, and you aren't in great condition, you will tire before the end and might even end up with uncontrollable cramps.

Analyzing Your Posing

One of the best ways of learning is by imitation. The same can be true in learning to pose. Young bodybuilders frequently study the routines of their idols and try to copy them. This can be valuable, but only if the bodybuilder you copy has the same sort of physique that you do.

If you have a Frank Zane or Franco Columbu type of body, you should not copy me. On the other hand, if you have the proportions of an Arnold Schwarzenegger, you should learn to take advantage of this, and not throw away your edge by doing the posing routine of a small, densely muscular bodybuilder.

I can't analyze your physique for you, but I can show you how I go about ascertaining what poses are right for me and which are not. By studying the process rather than the specific results, you can get an idea of how to apply this to your own developmental needs.

1. The Javelin-Thrower Pose

Poses can be athletic, aesthetic or muscular, and this pose is a little of each. I use this pose to give the impression of a Greek statue and to take advantage of my long proportions. Notice, however, that the effectiveness of this pose depends on having good biceps and good triceps—without development in these areas this pose would look ridiculous.

Also, this photograph points out the importance of flexing *all* your muscles in every pose. Even though this is primarily an upper body pose, I have my thighs and calves tensed to the maximum.

2. Abdominal Pose

Abdominal development has never been my strongest suit. Therefore, to display my abs, I like to do a pose that emphasizes the muscularity of my entire upper body and creates a wide look to the shoulders to make my waist seem even narrower. Notice how the powerful look of my arms, delts and pectorals complements my abdominal development.

And, once again, it is apparent that the legs must be flexed to enhance the overall effect of the pose.

3. Side Biceps Shot

This is an aesthetic way of
showing off the biceps which,
at the same time, emphasizes
the mass of the deltoids and
the upper arm and makes the
waist seem slender and narrow. I use this pose fre-
quently as a preliminary to a
full one-arm biceps shot.
Since this is a more aesthetic
pose, notice that I try to stay
looking relaxed—that makes
it even more dramatic when I
bring my right arm up into a
full biceps shot and really hit
the pose hard.

In this pose, and several
others, I like to turn slightly
to the side, twist, and not
face the camera directly. This
makes the waist look nar-
rower and keeps the poses
from seeming too "blocky."

4. Behind-the-Neck Biceps Shot

This is a good example of how many different ways there are to show off any body part. Here, I am flexing the biceps, but I have also revealed the serratus and intercostal muscles of the torso by placing one hand behind my head. This has also brought out the lats, emphasized by the V-shaped torso, and made my waist seem smaller.

Where you look can make a significant difference in any pose. Looking away from the biceps instead of toward them, I have given just the right tilt to my body and created a much more pleasing impression.

5. Most Muscular Pose

It is important to do a "most muscular" shot sometime during your presentation, but there are a number of ways of doing this pose. The traditional "crab" shot is, perhaps, the most impressive, but this variation is much more aesthetic.

I always do a slight hip twist in this pose, and work one arm against the other to bring out maximum striations in the arms and chest. Also, notice that I am not letting my face distort into an ugly look the way many bodybuilders do, but am keeping my face relaxed and smiling, so that I continue to relate to the audience even while putting out maximum effort.

6. Front Double Biceps

This is a standard, compulsory pose, and there is a good reason why. You really have to have the physique to look good doing this pose—no misdirection, no deception, no looking like a Greek Olympian. You have to have the arms, the serratus, intercostals, the works.

But see how I remember that the entire body is still on view, not just the biceps. My lats are spread, hips twisted slightly to minimize the waist, stomach held in, quadriceps and calves tensed. Also, in this photo and most of the others, I wear black trunks, since this does not draw attention to the midsection and so de-emphasizes the waist.

Using a Gym

Growing up in Austria, I remember how local craftsmen used to tell me, "A workman is only as good as his tools." The same thing can be said of bodybuilding.

The body is a highly complex mechanism, and you just can't train every muscle from every necessary angle with a few simple pieces of equipment. A bench, some free weights and a chinning bar can help you to build the fundamental structure that you need before you undertake advanced bodybuilding training, but at some point you will have to take advantage of the technological developments in exercise equipment that have helped bodybuilders obtain their present unbelievable competitive physiques.

With a large enough investment, you can actually have this kind of equipment in your home. But most people find it more economical and convenient to join a good gym. The right kind of gym will have more equipment than generally available to you at home, and it will have more different kinds. When I train at World Gym in Santa Monica, for instance, I have the advantage of using equipment that gym owner Joe Gold has designed and built himself. With all the great bodybuilders who train there, you know that a piece of equipment that doesn't feel right gets taken out in a hurry. Joe gets immediate feedback from the professionals, and this allows him to make corrections in short order.

This kind of feedback is essential in designing good exercise equipment. Most of the benches and machines you will find in any good gym are the products of years of trial and error experimentation on the part of bodybuildings and manufacturers.

Modern equipment manufacturers have learned that how equipment looks, how much chrome it carries, is not as important as how it feels—and you ascertain that by asking the people who use it.

When you first walk into a well-equipped gym, it might look as if much of the equipment is redundant, but this is not the case. You need a variety of exercises to keep surprising and shocking the muscles and to overcome the limitations of progressively diminishing returns from training. To accomplish that, you have to:

(1) Make the muscles do movements they are not used to;

(2) Make the muscles do movements they are used to in slightly different ways;

(3) Make the muscles work in familiar movements, but at unfamiliar angles;

(4) Work the body in such a way as to isolate certain muscles or muscle groups that you have previously worked in combination with others.

There are a number of pieces of equipment that help you do this. A few of them are:

(1) *Cable devices.* You work against the resistance of a cable, attached through a pulley to a stack of weights. With a machine like this, you can do Curls, Flys, Tricep Push-downs, Rowing, Lat Pull-downs, Lateral Raises and a host of other exercises which almost—but not quite—duplicate the movements you would do with other pieces of equipment.

(2) *Fixed-weight machines.* Barbells and dumbbells are "free weights"; any time you lift a weight that is held by a machine and moves in a fixed plane, you get a different kind of feeling. You no longer need technique to balance and lift the

weight nor such complex timing, which allows you to work on pure strength. However, since the machine and not your own joints is determining the plane of movement, some disadvantageous stresses can develop in the body.

(3) *Variable-leverage machines.* Whenever you lift a weight, because your limbs are really sets of levers, the "leverage" or mechanical advantage constantly changes, making the weight relatively lighter or heavier at various points in the lift because you are effectively stronger or weaker at those points. Some fixed-weight machines ignore this, and the weight remains the same throughout the limit of movement. Others use variable cams or levers to change the leverage, making the weight heavier when you are mechanically stronger, and lighter when you are lifting through a weak point. These machines are increasingly popular, but bodybuilders are somewhat leery of them, since it has been shown that the so-called "strength curve" built into these machines often does not match the strength curve of a trained bodybuilder. It is designed, instead, to conform to the physical requirements of the average man. Bodybuilders use some of these machines for specialized movements, but tend to rely more normally on free weights, cables and other fixed-leverage types of training.

(4) *Benches.* A good gym usually has a wide variety of benches—flat benches, incline benches, decline benches, benches with a rack behind the neck for Shoulder Presses, with a support in back for Tricep Presses, with a support in front for Preacher Bench Curls. This is a great example of how beneficial it can be to simply do the same exercises from slightly different angles, or to substitute dumbbells for a barbell or vice-versa. There is no limit except your imagination to the use you can make of benches.

Any movement you can do with free weights can be duplicated on a machine. That doesn't make the machines superior, however. Most bodybuilders agree that no champion has ever been developed using machines exclusively. There is something about the feel of free weights, the freedom of movement allowed the joints, the feedback given to your kinesiological sense that gives superior results.

Certain muscles and body parts are difficult to train without using some machines. Legs are a good example. I have always done Squats and Lunges with free weights, but included Leg Presses, Leg Curls and Extensions and Calf Raises into the workout done on various kinds of machines. A good bodybuilder uses as wide a variety of equipment as it takes to get the job done.

The Bodybuilder As Pioneer
For the first year or several years that you train for competition bodybuilding you will be relying, for the most part, on techniques and strategies that have been developed by and for other people. This is normal. In any sport, the first step is to learn fundamentals. However, once you achieve an advanced level, there is no longer any clear-cut path to follow. You have to break your own trail.

Nobody knows what the potentials and limitations of the human body really are. Athletes are running faster, jumping further, getting stronger. And bodybuilders are discovering potentials in the body that science and medicine had no idea existed. The body-

builders who are doing this are not following anybody else's prescription for training; they are making it up as they go along. But their decisions are based on years of experience and experimentation. They are anything but arbitrary.

Down the road, you are going to have to decide what works best for you. It may not be what works best for me. That knowledge is slow in coming, and you have to pay very close attention to what your body is doing. Some good bodybuilders write down everything they do in every training session and every morsel of food that they put in their mouths; others do it strictly by feel. Again, individual differences determine your ultimate strategy.

Don't try to "reinvent the wheel" right off—learn from what we who have gone before you have discovered. But keep in mind that these are not firm rules, but suggested guidelines. At some point, if you want to go beyond the mediocre, you are going to have to discover what the needs of your own body are, and how to individualize your diet and training to develop your full potential.

PART IX
DIET AND NUTRITION

Back to Basics

Everywhere I go I am constantly asked questions about diet and nutrition. Although primarily people are interested in losing weight, there is a growing awareness of the importance of nutrition in staying healthy.

Most people use the word "diet" to mean eating to lose weight. Actually, the word just refers to a particular pattern of eating. If you eat correctly, and combine that with a sufficient amount of rigorous exercise, losing excess weight and maintaining a healthy body weight should not be a problem.

But the public is so bombarded nowadays with conflicting opinions, claims and promises regarding diet and nutrition that most don't know what to believe. One expert wants you to eat a diet high in protein and low in carbohydrate, while another comes along and points out that this kind of diet can be too high in fats and cholesterol, and so he recommends just the opposite.

What I recommend is going back to basics. We all tend to want to have our cake and eat it, but the fact is that basic nutrition is not all that mysterious, and most people need to follow the old tried-and-true rules that all of us learned in high school about what makes for a balanced, nutritious diet, rather than trying to follow the latest fad diet.

The Nutrition Factor

To start at the beginning, the body uses food for a number of things. One of the most important is the production of energy. The energy we consume and the energy we use in exercise is measured in units called "calories," which is actually a term that refers to heat production.

But the body also uses food to build, maintain and repair tissue, as well as to provide the nutrients required for a variety of vital functions. These are rather complex needs, because physical systems are themselves complicated, and so it takes a variety of foods to fulfill these requirements.

The food we eat comes in three basic forms:

(1) *Protein* is the body's basic structural material.

(2) *Carbohydrate* converts to sugar in the body for the production of energy.

(3) *Fat* is the most energy-efficient form of food, and so any extra energy is stored for later use in this form.

But the biochemistry of the body is much more complicated than this, and these food forms have a variety of different uses and interact with one another in numerous ways. But you don't have to be a biochemist to learn to eat well, so let's try to keep it simple.

Vitamins and minerals are nutrients present in the body in very small amounts, because they usually operate only as catalysts, "triggers" that allow other processes to take place. When we don't have a sufficient amount of certain vitamins, deficiencies develop that can range from the very minor to the very serious.

A lot of people take vitamin supplementation these days. Ideally, the only reason to take vitamin supplements is to cure a vitamin deficiency. Vitamins seem to operate in such a way that once you have enough, more doesn't do any good. But there is a controversy concerning just how much is enough.

Stress, processed foods, pollution, cigarettes, alcohol and a number of other factors rob the body of vitamins. Some experts say that eating a balanced diet is sufficient to counter these influences, while other disagree and prescribe moderate to massive supplementation. There is no clear consensus.

The same holds true for minerals. Minerals are the stuff of which our planet is made, and we share the need for a number of minerals such as calcium, zinc, iron and so on. Those who claim we should all be taking mineral supplementation, as well as extra vitamins, believe that too frequently the soil in which our food is grown has itself been depleted of minerals and is no longer sufficiently nutritious. Again, there is no general agreement.

The Balanced Diet

Protein is most easily obtained from eating animal tissue, but many vegetables contain a lot of protein as well. Certain meats, such as lamb, beef and pork, are good sources of protein, but high in fat, too. So a lot of people are cutting back on these meats in their diet and adding more poultry and fish, which contain much less fat.

Vegetables contain a variety of vitamins and minerals, and themselves are predominately carbohydrate. Carbohydrate has gotten bad press recently, because people confuse the general term with one specific kind of carbohydrate—namely, sugar. The complex carbohydrates found in broccoli, potatoes and other vegetables are high in nutrition, relatively low in calories, and far better for you than the simple carbohydrates such as table sugar.

Fruits are also carbohydrate, but are closer in nature to sugar than most vegetables. They lack protein, but they are good sources of a number of other nutrients. Fructose, the sugar found in fruit, is many times sweeter than processed sugar, so it gives you more sweetness per calorie than high-sugar desserts.

A U.S. Government study recently made the following recommendations for balancing your diet:

Protein	12%
Carbohydrate	58%
Fat	30%

Breaking this down into actual amounts, the suggestion is:

Protein	1 gram per 2.2 lbs. of body weight
Carbohydrate	minimum of about 80 grams, more with exercise

Most athletes, bodybuilders among them, prefer larger amounts of protein, more like 1 gram for every pound of body weight. But there are experts who believe that we eat too much protein already, and not nearly enough carbohydrate. Everyone accepts that eating too much fat is harmful.

Carbohydrates are important to the body in many ways. It is, for example, the only energy source the brain can draw upon. Too little carbohydrate and the brain cannot function properly. When you exercise heavily, you tend to use up carbohydrates, so you need to eat enough to fuel both your exercise and your nervous system.

Carbohydrates also combine with fat in the biochemical cycle that produces energy to fuel the muscles. Therefore, very low or zero carbohydrate diets tend to be self-defeating, because they inhibit the metabolism of fat. But I'll get into that a little deeper shortly.

The important thing to keep in mind is that all of these nutrients are *interrelated*. They all work together to keep you healthy and functioning. When there is an overabundance of copper, for example, it will result in lower levels of zinc. So whether you are trying to gain, lose or maintain weight, stick to eating a balanced diet and a variety of different foods, and avoid any advice that tells you different.

Eating to Lose Weight

At the most basic level, your body accumulates fat when you eat more than you need, and it loses fat when you use more energy that you have ingested in your food. When energy in equals energy out, there is no change in body weight.

Individuals differ considerably in how efficiently they digest food. They also differ in how active they are, and in how many calories they burn up through exercise. But we can generalize and say that one pound of fat contains about 3500 calories for most people.

Since calories are both a measurement of how much energy fat contains and the energy cost of various kinds of exercise, there are obviously two factors we can manipulate to produce a negative caloric balance. . . .

(1) We can eat less.
(2) We can exercise more.

Ideally, to lose weight and stay healthy you should do *both*.

Exercising for Weight Loss

When people get heavier, they tend to be less active. Also, people who use up less energy tend to get heavier—the two work hand in hand. I've seen studies that show a fat person playing tennis will tend to be energy-conservative, taking as few steps as possible and only moving when it is absolutely necessary. The thin person on the other side of the net, however, will run around and have a great time, and thus use up a lot more calories than his heavier opponent.

Some nutritionists avoid telling fat people they should exercise, because they believe that these individuals will tend to get discouraged, being forced into unfamiliar activity, and go off their weight-loss program. That may be true, but there is little likelihood of permanent weight loss without an alteration of exercise patterns.

Exercise doesn't seem to help much, many people feel. After all, if you run a mile, you only burn up about 100 calories. But do that every day—and it takes less than 10 minutes—and you are talking about the energy equivalent of 10 pounds a year. Add a moderate reduction in food intake, and you can easily lose 20 pounds a year on this program. Most people would be more than satisfied if they could lose that much that easily.

So exercise is invaluable in controlling weight, but only if it is kept up over a long period of time. The weight training I've given you in this program will help; so will playing sports, riding a bicycle and any other kind of exercise.

Just remember, weight control is a matter of balance between intake and expenditure—don't try it using only half of the equation.

The Low-Cal Diet

When you cut down on your caloric intake, you lose weight. This is assuming that you don't limit your food intake to the point where you begin to lack some of the needed nutrients. If this happens, your level of energy expenditure tends to drop, your metabolism does not function with its customary efficiency, and you don't lose the weight you intend to.

Trying to lose weight too fast is self-defeating and unhealthy. In most circumstances, a 2-pound-per-week loss is as much as you should hope for. Any more than this and it usually requires such sacrifices or simply alterations in your normal habits that you can't keep on with it for very long.

There are any number of charts and tables that will tell you what your optimum caloric requirements might be, but the best way to tell is to check and see if what you are eating is causing you to gain, maintain or lose—keeping in mind that changes in muscle mass can also affect the scale.

As you cut back from this equilibrium level, and increase your exercise, your body will dip into its fat reserves to obtain the needed energy. The trick is not to cut back so far that you deprive yourself of your daily nutritional needs. At this point, all you need is patience. The body will go about its business at its own rate, and no use hurrying it.

But keep in mind that the body is a living organism, not a machine, and its processes do not always proceed at uniform rates. For example, you might go two weeks hardly losing any weight, then lose a whole lot in just a few days. One reason for this is that for every gram of fat your body metabolizes, more than a gram of water is produced as a byproduct. This water stays in your system for some time before being cycled out, so the loss of fat is not immediately noticeable.

How Much Is Enough?

Being lean is healthier than being heavy—assuming that the behavior that keeps you lean is not itself unhealthy. But just how lean is enough? The average man in this country has a relative body fat content of about 15 percent. This is not considered fat, unless you are an athlete and can't afford even that much fat on your body. Most good athletes have body fat contents under 10 percent, and when I was in contest shape during my competition years, my relative body fat was in the neighborhood of 3–4 percent.

We all have a tendency to put on weight as we get older. The metabolism, for example, slows down by 10 calories per day per year after the age of 25–30. This means that the average man could expect to gain 10 pounds between his 30th and 40th birthdays if he made no other adjustments.

Also, age tends to make us sedentary. We get involved in family, business, social obligations and the like, and we don't automatically get out and exercise as much as we did when we were kids.

But we can alter that pattern, and exercise more. We can acknowledge that it is necessary to adjust our caloric intake to reflect our lifestyles. When we do this, our weight will tend to drop to acceptable levels and stay there.

Each person has to decide for himself how much fat is acceptable on his own body. If you can pinch a large layer of fat around your waistline, then it is probably time to do something about it. Also, as you begin to train with weights and become more conscious of your body, you may well decide you don't want to be "average," that you would rather be in above-average condition.

At that point, by using your knowledge of exercise, diet and nutrition, you can take steps to recreate yourself in whatever image you decide is desirable.

Diet Hints and Shortcuts

If you follow the energy-in/energy-out program, you will have little trouble keeping your weight under control. But there are a few ways to make it easier:

(1) *Control your portions.* Use a calorie counter, measuring cup and kitchen scale so that you know how much you are putting on your plate. Keep it down to a dull roar.

(2) *Fill up with bulk foods.* Foods like lettuce and other salad vegetables have little caloric content but can fill you up. In planning your meals, make it easy on yourself and include some of these bulk foods.

(3) *Cut back on sugar.* Table sugar, ice cream, processed foods, cake and all the rest of these foods are high in calories, lacking in nutrition. They bounce your blood-sugar level up and down and play havoc with your appetite. Successful weight control depends to a great extent on your ability to reduce and control your sugar consumption.

(4) *Don't get hungry.* Going without food and developing a feeling of deprivation just makes you overeat further down the line. Better to never skip a meal and, when you get hungry between meals, eat something—an apple, a small salad, something that will fill you up and satisfy your appetite without adding too much to your overall caloric intake.

(5) *Alcohol counts.* Cocktails, beer, wine and all other alcoholic beverages add calories to your diet without providing much in the way of nutrition. Take them into account when you are keeping score, and cut back if you can.

(6) *Don't ruin your food.* A potato has only about 100 calories, but becomes a real threat covered in butter and sour cream. A nice salad can be ruined by putting 6 tablespoons of oil dressing on it (at 100 calories a tablespoon). Breading meat, French sauces, frying in oil and all other manner of adding unnecessary calories to your diet should be avoided.

(7) *Take your time.* Eat slowly, enjoy your food, and give your body a chance to recognize that your hunger has been satisfied. Starting with a salad before you get to the main course is one way to avoid overeating.

The Food Diary

It is often hard to recall exactly what you have eaten on any given day, and thus difficult to pinpoint where problems in your diet may be occurring.

A way around this is to write down everything you eat and, if you have the patience, actually look up the caloric values of your daily food intake and add up the total.

This can become very tedious, so it is hard to do every day, but keeping a diary even once or twice a week can be extremely valuable in helping you learn to modify your eating behavior.

Gaining Weight

We hear so much about the problems of the obese in our culture, that many times we tend to forget that there are lots of people who have the opposite problem, that of how to gain weight.

Many young boys who are skinny are in such a hurry to gain weight that they overeat and end up becoming quite fat a few years later. If your slenderness is due to a lack of body fat, be grateful.

The cure for painful skinnyness is to increase the body's muscle mass. This, however, takes time, as I have already pointed out. And it is probably likely, unless you are very young, that your lack of muscle mass is genetic, so that you will put on mass more slowly than most. But hard training will change the shape, contour and look of your body, even before you have gained a significant amount of muscle, and I think you will really like the way that makes you look.

PART X
WEIGHT TRAINING
FOR ALL AGES

The Ages of Man

William Shakespeare tells us that the "ages of man" are seven. There is the infant, then the whining schoolboy, followed by the young lover, then the soldier, the middle-aged and successful justice, to be succeeded by the enfeebled old man. Finally, "second childishness and mere oblivion, / Sans teeth, sans eyes, sans taste, sans every thing."

Today age no longer has to mean automatic deterioration, but forestalling deterioration involves a great deal of effort, dedication and attention to physical training. Especially weight training. So this is how I would describe the process:

First—there is the infant, possessed of a rapidly growing body. By the trial and effort of movement, he grows strong and learns coordination. At this age, working against the resistance of his own body is enough to ensure proper development. During the late pre-adolescent period, the time is right to introduce calesthenic movements, gymnastics and aerobic training.

Second—there is the adolescent, his body flooded by hormones, growing in both size and muscle mass. At this point, the physical structure is ready to support some moderately heavy weight training. However, the adolescent has bones which are not fully hardened, and so it must be remembered that his manly muscles are capable of lifting heavier weights than his youthful skeleton can, or should, really support.

Third—there is the young man, the athlete, whose body has matured and is, in many ways, at its all-around physical peak. He is the football and bas-

James M. Riehman: A marketing and public relations executive

ketball player, the 20-game winner, the crack pilot, the infantryman enduring enormous hardships in the field. His body can take whatever amounts of stress he is in condition to handle, and this includes training with very heavy weight.

Fourth—there is the mature man, in his thirties, who may have lost some of his cardiovascular capability but who has learned to compensate for this by becoming more economic and efficient in his movements, the gift of experience. Yet he also continues to grow stronger and can work with as great an amount of resistance as he chooses—limited only by his ability to stay in top condition.

Fifth—there is the career man, the successful businessman or executive. He has reached and probably passed his athletic peak, and now he is concerned with improving his health and maintaining his strength. At this age, so many men succumb to diseases of age and stress like stroke and cardiac problems that an appropriate program of moderate exercise is even more important than ever.

Sixth—there is the retired man, the man of sixty, concerned that he retain the use of all his faculties so as to fully enjoy his new leisure. The metabolism is slower at this age, the body slower to recover from injury or illness, but it continues to respond to exercise, especially a program of resistance movements to counteract the tendency of muscle to atrophy with age.

Seventh—there is old age, but not the kind that Will must have seen around him daily. This is old age accompanied by strength, mobility and independence. And this is achieved by continuing to be active, to walk and swim, to play games, and to use the muscles against some kind of resistance. At this time of life there is usually little need for barbells and dumbbells, but often the elderly find that the exercise devices employed to help rehabilitate orthopedic patients are also valuable in overcoming the limitations of arthritis and the effects of long periods of inactivity.

Weight Training for Every Age

The very young and the very old need resistance training as much as anyone, but it should be of a different sort. And this makes sense because as we get older our minds change every bit as much as our bodies. For instance, at age fifteen I wanted to become so big people wouldn't believe it, and that's what I trained for; now, I am concerned with staying fit and healthy, so I have adapted my training to suit my current goals.

That is what everyone needs to do. Resistance training is always important, since it conforms to the needs of the muscle structure and this doesn't change no matter how old or young you are. But not everyone should or would want to lift very heavy weight. It depends on age, circumstances and personal predilection. But whether you use heavy or light weight, there is no substitute for making your muscles work against the stress of resistance.

Young children, before they have developed physical maturity, should stay away from heavy weight. I started lifting at fifteen, and that was about right. Older people should certainly not just jump precipitately into resistance training without a long period of conditioning and under a doctor's supervision. Everyone in between should use common sense in determining how strenuous a program is right for them. Remember, you don't just start tossing weights around at age fifty if you have done nothing athletic for twenty years. But you can work up to it slowly, and get all the benefits.

A Final Word

I'd like to tell you about a man who used to train in the same gym where I trained back in Austria. He was quite a bit older than anybody else in the gym, probably somewhere in his late forties. Normally, as far as my teenage friends and I were concerned, anyone over forty was too old to be bothered with, but this man was hardly typical of what we thought of as middle-aged.

First of all, he was big, with a hard, defined physique that would have suited a man twenty years younger. And, in spite of his age, he trained as hard as any of us, although with a calm, deliberate manner that contrasted with our own boisterous enthusiasm. But he knew a lot, and so we watched him and learned.

One day I ran across his picture in an old magazine from the forties. He had been about twenty pounds heavier in those days and, according to the magazine, had been very successful in European physique competition. This really caught my interest because there was nothing I cared more about than winning bodybuilding contests. Since he was still in such good shape, I couldn't imagine why he had stopped competing. To me, that would be like stopping breathing. So one day I summoned up the courage to ask him.

"Arnold," he told me, "when I was your age, I wanted the things you want. To be massive, to win contests. I was very competitive. After a while, when I had won my share, I began to compete against myself. I wanted to develop the absolutely perfect physique, and I drove myself almost past endurance to achieve that."

He stopped for a moment and looked up at a poster of Steve Reeves that was hung on the wall. An old rival, and you could see the spark of competition still lingered in his eyes.

"Then I got married," he went on, "I had a good job offer from a sporting goods firm and, when the kids came, there just wasn't any room left in my life for competition training. I hardly worked out for years, until one day I looked in the mirror. Suddenly I saw the sagging chest, the belly, the softness around the chin. I almost couldn't recognize the man I was looking at. I went back into training that afternoon. Since then, no matter how busy I get, I find the time to get in my workouts."

I suppose he saw the puzzled look on my face and realized he was talking to a teenage boy who lacked the experience to fully understand what he was saying. He stopped talking and smiled.

"I still compete, Arnold," he said, clapping me on the shoulder, "only now it's against that." He pointed behind me, then turned and went back to his workout. I turned and looked.

He had pointed at the clock.

Free posing—Mr. Olympia 1980

Neal Nordlinger

Mr. Olympia lineup

Final pose-off between Boyer Coe, Arnold, and Chris Dickerson

Victory pose after winning Mr. Olympia 1980

Victory pose at the Opera House in Sydney, Australia, after winning seventh Mr. Olympia title.

Index

PHOTO CREDITS—

All photographs were taken by
   Peter Brenner except the
   following:
John Balik, 192
Albert Busek, 208, 210, 237, 238
Caruso, 219, 220
Bill Dobbins, 17, 233
Robert Gardner, 205, 213
Neal Nordlinger, 236, 239
Art Zeller, 15, 119–204, 206–
   212, 218, 221–223, 226